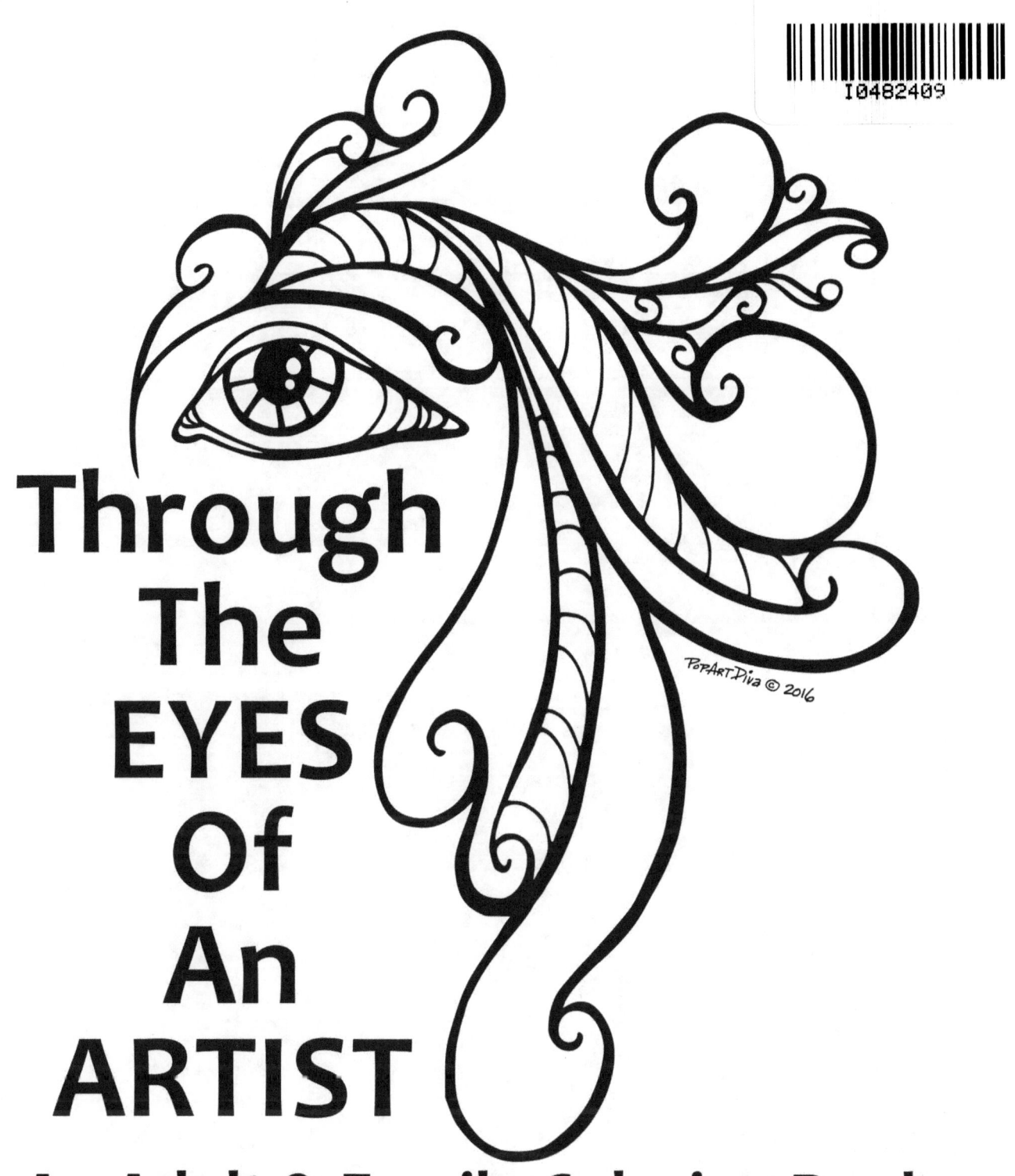

Through The EYES Of An ARTIST

An Adult & Family Coloring Book of Fantasy Faces

by Pop Art Diva aka Terri Dennis

Through The EYES Of An ARTIST
An Adult & Family Coloring Book of Fantasy Faces
by Pop Art Diva aka Terri Dennis

A unique, one-of-a-kind coloring book featuring women's eyes and faces morphing into all nature of earthly and fantasy creatures and designs from abstracts, butterflies, fish and sea critters, dragonflies, birds, flowers and even a skull and a cosmic view of space. All seen *"through the eyes"* of an artist.

WHAT'S INSIDE?

* **31 Beautiful, *HAND DRAWN* Coloring Pages**
* **All Pages are Single Sided**
* **15 Vertical Images and 15 Horizontal Images, *PLUS* the Cover Art!**
* **Skill levels are easy to moderately detailed.**
* **Well defined boundaries to make it easy to "color inside the lines"**
* **Includes Coloring Tips, Coloring Medium Charts and Medium Testing Pages!**

All of the coloring pages within this book are completely **hand drawn**. Done in ink, on paper and in nearly all cases, directly inked with *no preliminary sketching* done. I did not use any digital drawing processes at all when creating these images except for the clean up stage where I correct noogies (my word for mistakes or a slip of the pen.) You can even see progress videos as I drew many of the designs on my Facebook page at **Facebook.com/ColoringLifeHappy**.

What does this mean? It means that these are not perfect, and they're not meant to be. Nothing hand-drawn is perfect and it shouldn't be. The whole point of not using digital drawing tools is to leave in the charm of the artist's imperfections and, at the same time, include a little piece of the artist's soul.

I can, and do, create art completely digitally, I did for years professionally, which is why I wanted to get the pen and the paper back in my hands again and sit down and draw the way I was taught to draw. For me, personally, it is tremendously satisfying to have that physical contact with my art tools again. These drawings have given me many hours of artistic pleasure after having been separated from my art by bits and bytes for many years. I hope they bring equal measure of joy to you.

I love drawing eyes and faces but not JUST eyes and faces. Heck, I just like to draw, but it's always more fun if I can let my imagination run loose and that is what I did with these drawings. I used what I call a direct inking process, no pre-conceived idea or design. Starting with the eyes and part of a face, I then let the drawing tell me what it wanted to be and, with pen in hand, happily followed along. If you are surprised by these designs, imagine my surprise at what ended up on my sketch pad at the end of an illustration session. It was great fun to see my menagerie grow as I created the book and I hope you have as much fun coloring the images as I did creating them.

Enjoy and - always - *Color Life Happy!*

Terri Dennis, aka Pop Art Diva

OTHER COLORING BOOKS BY
Pop Art Diva - Terri Dennis - The Martini Diva:

DIY COLORING BOOK
An Adult Do It Yourself Coloring Book
For Anyone & Everyone Who Wants To Be An Artist

COLOR YOUR COCKTAILS
An Adult Coloring Book with Cocktail Recipes

MANDALAS & MOTIVATION Coloring Book
Color Yourself Calm, Inspired and Happy

COCKTAIL BOOKS BY
The Martini Diva, Terri Dennis

How to Practice The ZEN of COCKTAILS
A Beginner's Guide to Creative Cocktails at Home

The Martini Diva's HALLOWEEN MARTINIS & MUNCHIES BOOK
31 Spooky Halloween Martinis Paired with Halloween Munchies

The MERRY MARTINI MIXOLOGY BOOK
24 Holiday Martinis with Seasonal Spirit

VALENTINE MARTINIS
Love Potion Libations for Lovers

Copyright © 2016 Pop Art Diva, Terri Dennis
All rights reserved.
ISBN: 1535188022
ISBN-13: 978-1535188029

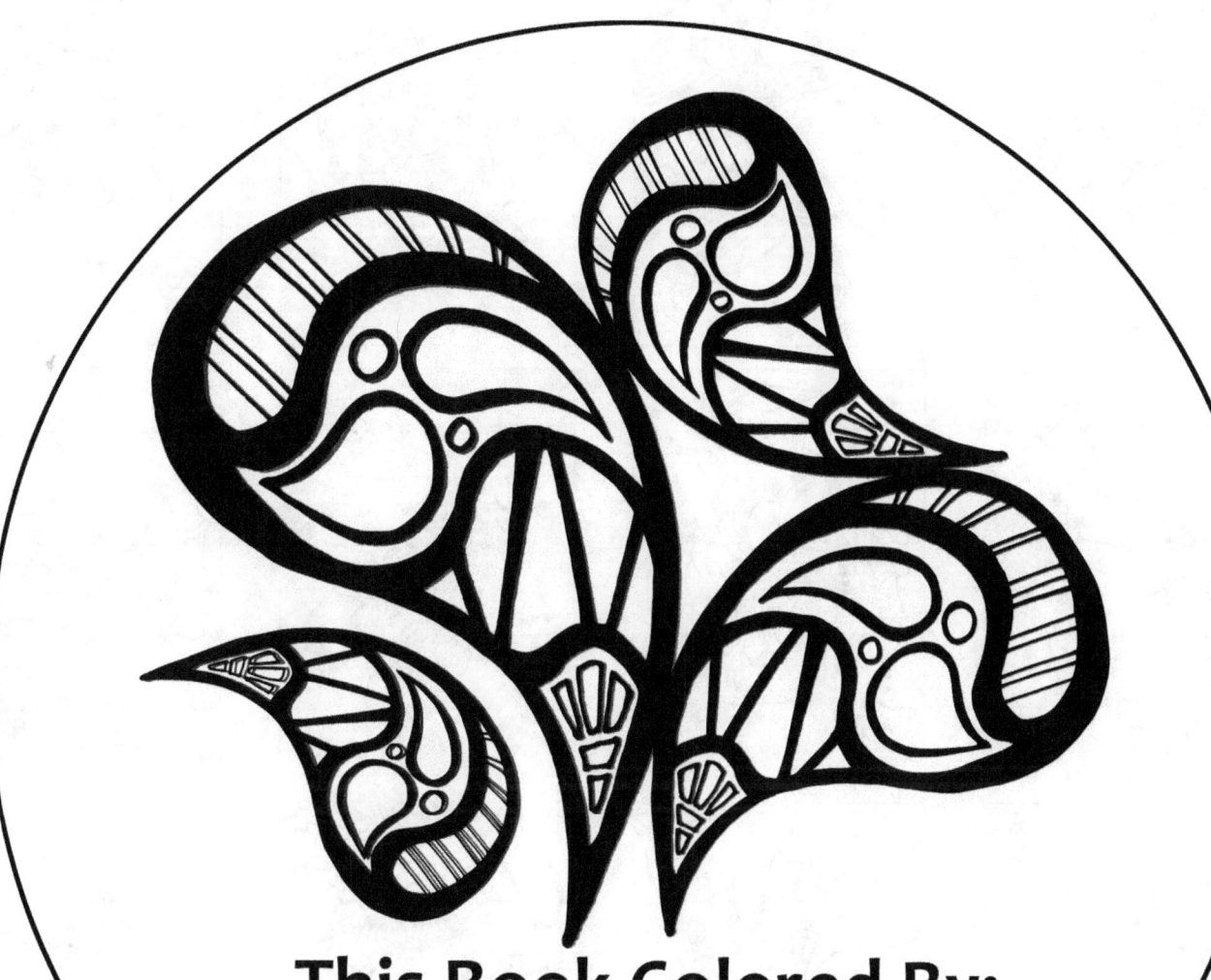

This Book Colored By:

_____

COLORING PAGE SAMPLES
Page 1 of 2 - 16 Verticals

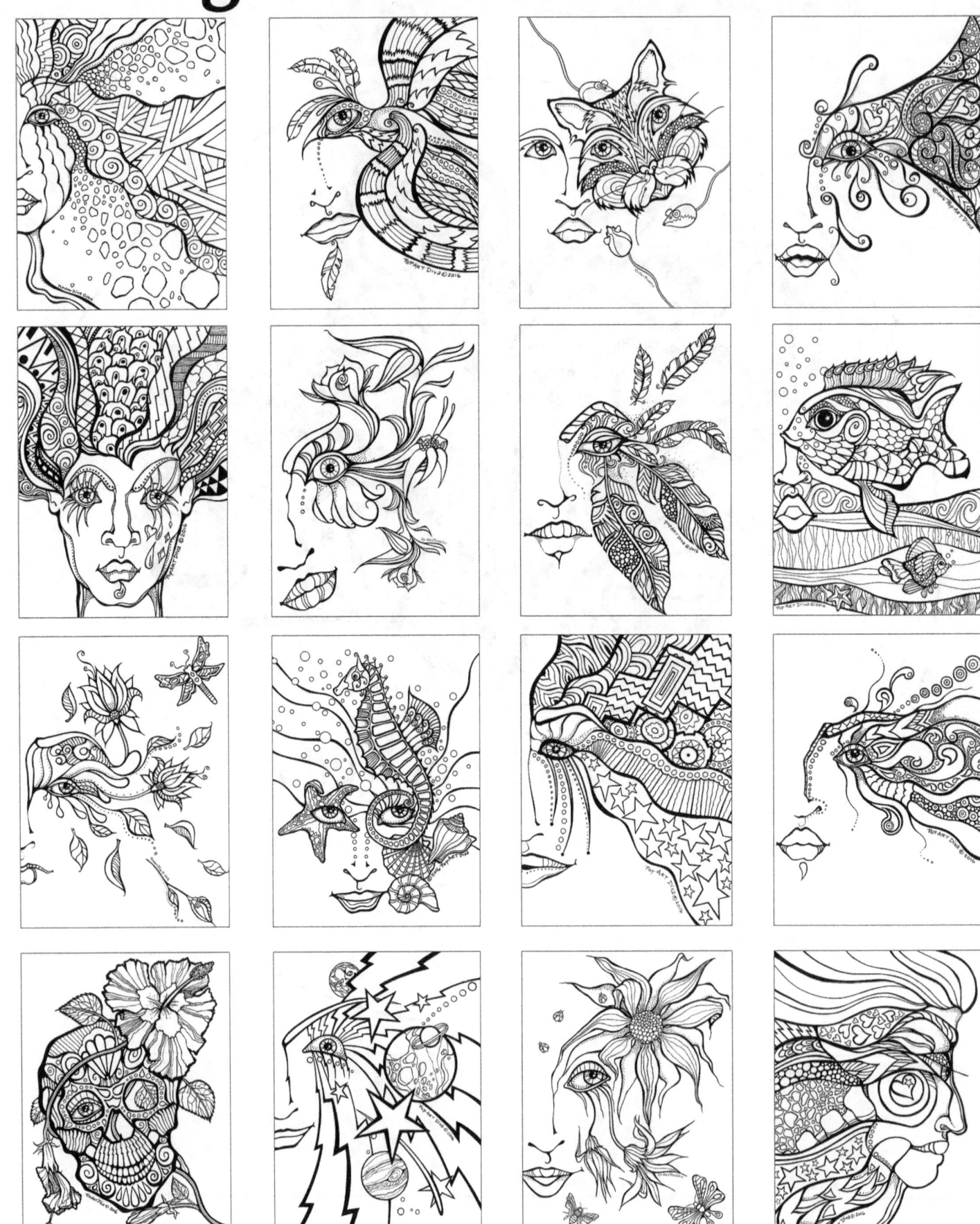

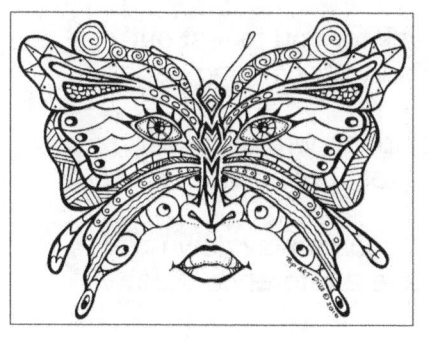
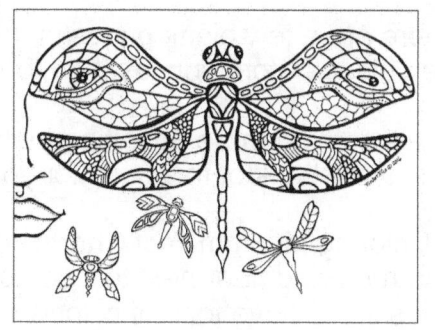
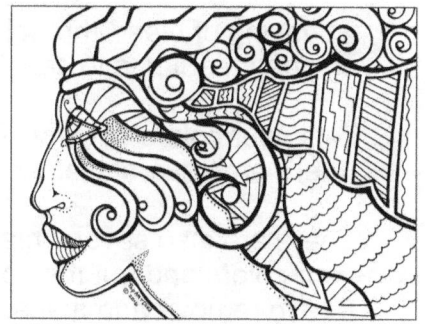
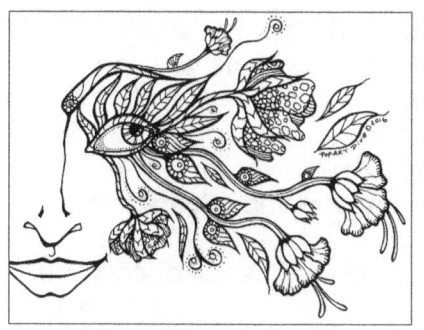
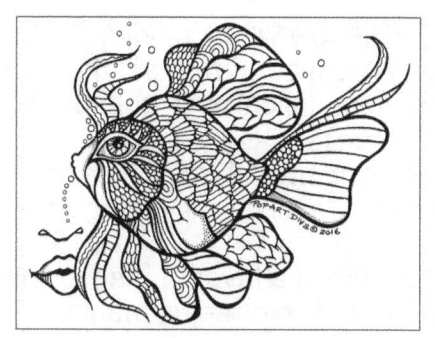
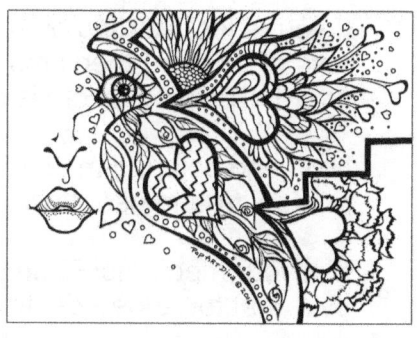
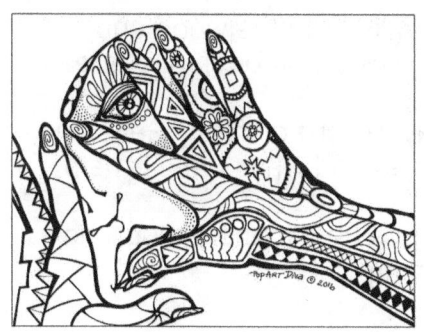
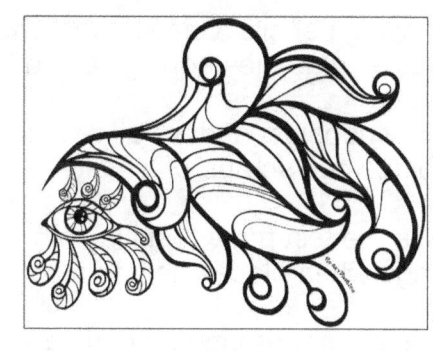
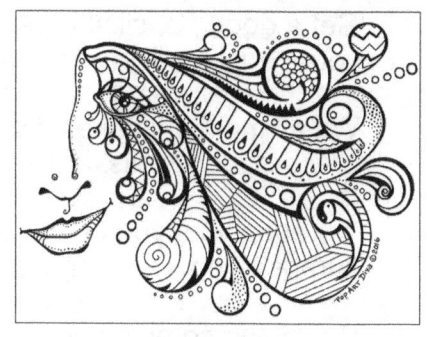
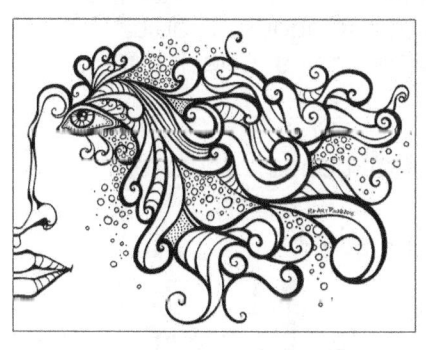
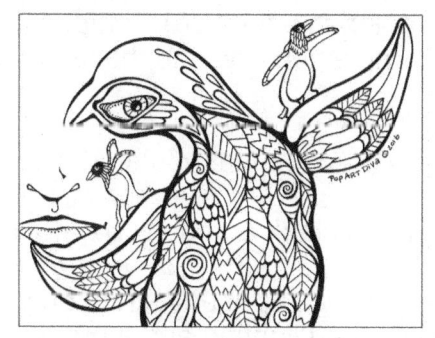
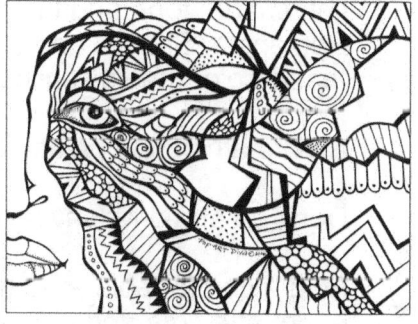
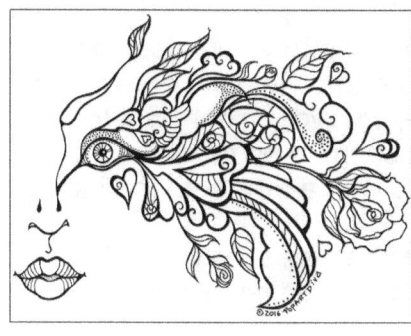
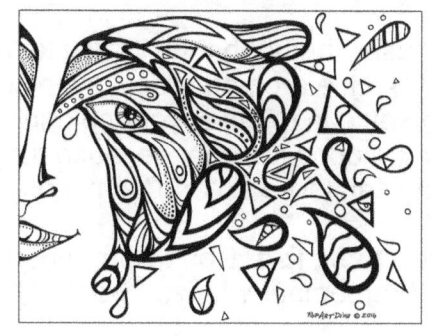
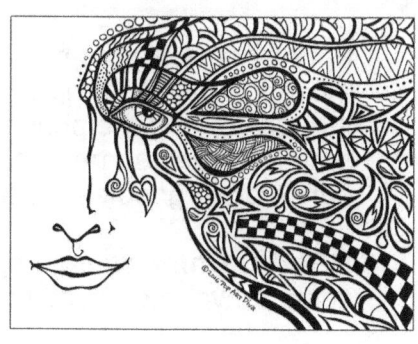

SOME (HOPEFULLY) HELPFUL COLORING TIPS:

Each coloring page is singled sided for convenience if you like to remove your pages. BUT if you like to leave your pages in the book it's **always wise to place a piece of heavy card stock behind your work**. This stops bleed-through of markers and impression marks from pencils.

Speaking of bleed-through, there are a few blank pages in the back for you to test out coloring mediums to see if they bleed before you lay them down on your coloring page.

Test your colors out first! There's nothing more upsetting than using the wrong color! There are several blank pages at the back of this book for your to test out colors.

There are also several blank Coloring Medium Test Charts where you can lay down your colors and put the color name or number next to it so you have a reference. Feel free to remove and make copies if you have tons of colors!

If you're just starting out and don't know what coloring medium you like best, get small sets of different mediums and try them out. *Then* get the best coloring mediums you can afford. Blending colors is much more difficult with cheap mediums.

High end coloring mediums are wonderful - I'm a Prismacolor and Copic lover myself - but feel free to use those crayons! Crayons really bring home the joy of being a kid again!

Mix your mediums! Example: Lay down a layer of marker then use colored pencil or crayons over that for added depth, texture and color adjustments.

Get a good pencil sharpener if using pencils. Cheap sharpeners will shred the wood and your pencils will break much easier, plus they don't give you that nice point for smaller areas.

We all make mistakes, I call mine noogies, and we all need a way to correct them. Get some erasers for pencils, an x-acto blade can scrape off smaller ooopsies and white pencils help.

Try out colors you don't like! Use the test pages and lay other colors next to them, you'll be surprised how a color can change when placed next to a contrasting color.

Download some color charts. Colors are grouped by primary, secondary, tertiary, warm, cool, tint, shade, tone and the basic color schemes are Complementary, Analogous, Triadic, Rectangle, Square and Split-Complementary. And those are just the basics. Check out "basic color theory" online.

Create a coloring palette for your piece before you start. Use the test pages for this too.

Don't be afraid to leave some areas blank and don't be afraid to use black!

Find a comfortable area where you won't put any strain on your body. Many folks color for hours at a time and a good chair, good lighting and a proper position for your coloring platform are all important to enjoying your coloring sessions.

Put on some of your favorite music, the boob tube or just let nature sing to you but set the mood for your coloring session. A little aromatherapy is a nice touch too. Get your drink, grab the remote and the phone and settle in to enjoy your coloring. Oh, btw, you might want to grab a toy and some treats for the doggy or kitty because they all seem to be fascinated by our coloring goodies. Bailey, my cat, loves to "add" to my drawings with a few teeth marks.

RELAX! Coloring is supposed to be fun! Don't worry about anyone else's work, don't compare yourself to others and remember why you wanted to color in the first place!

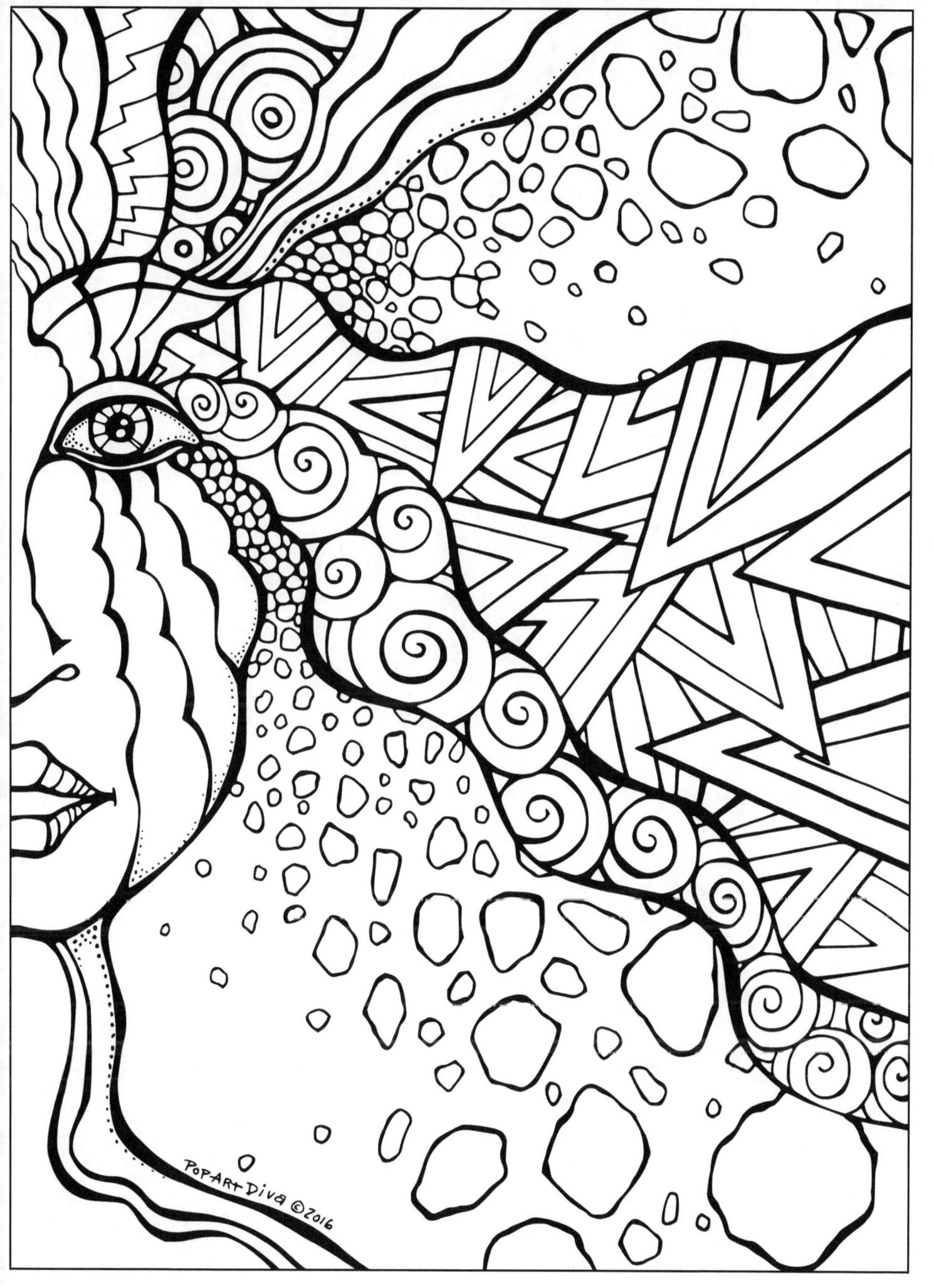

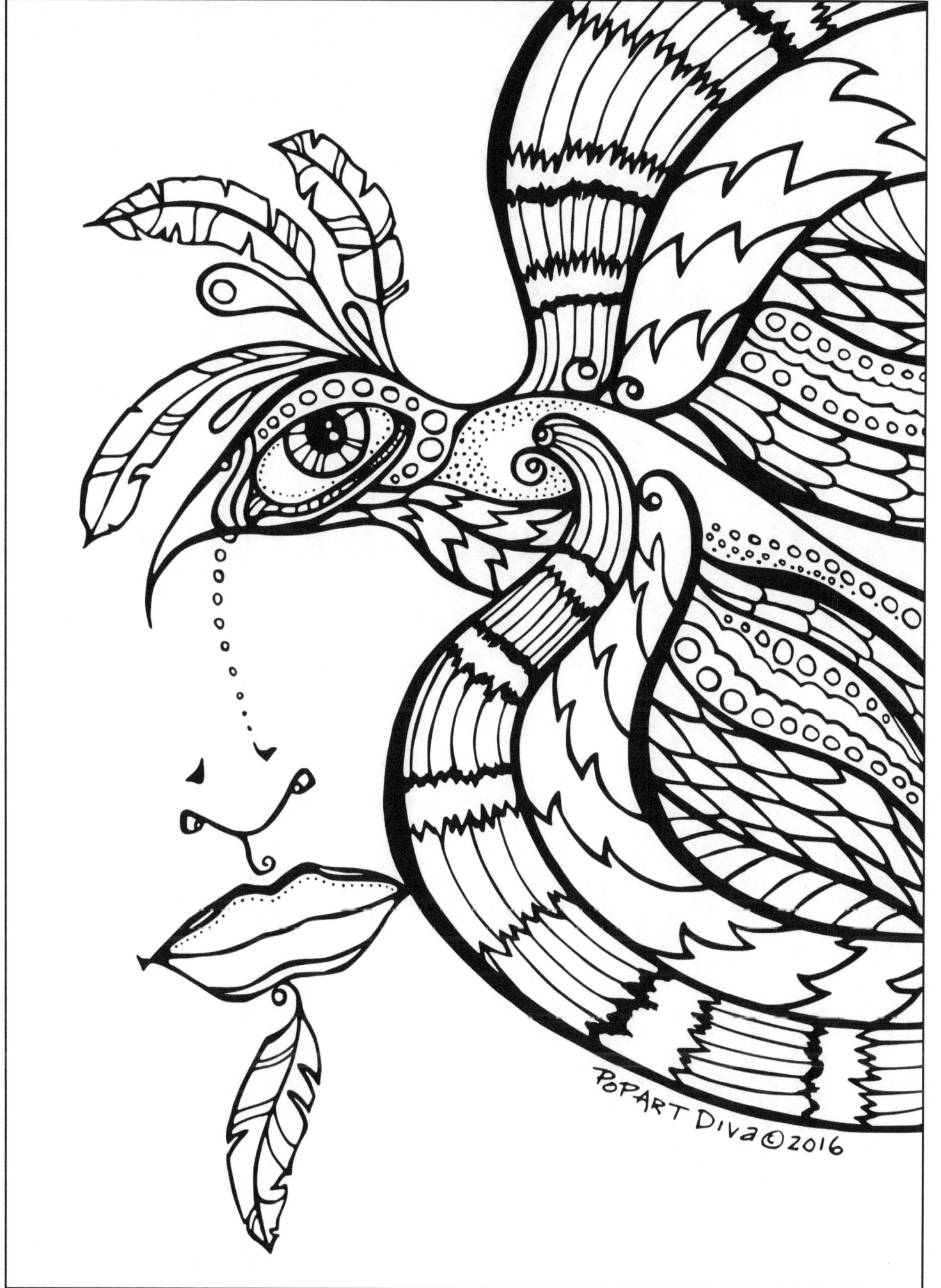

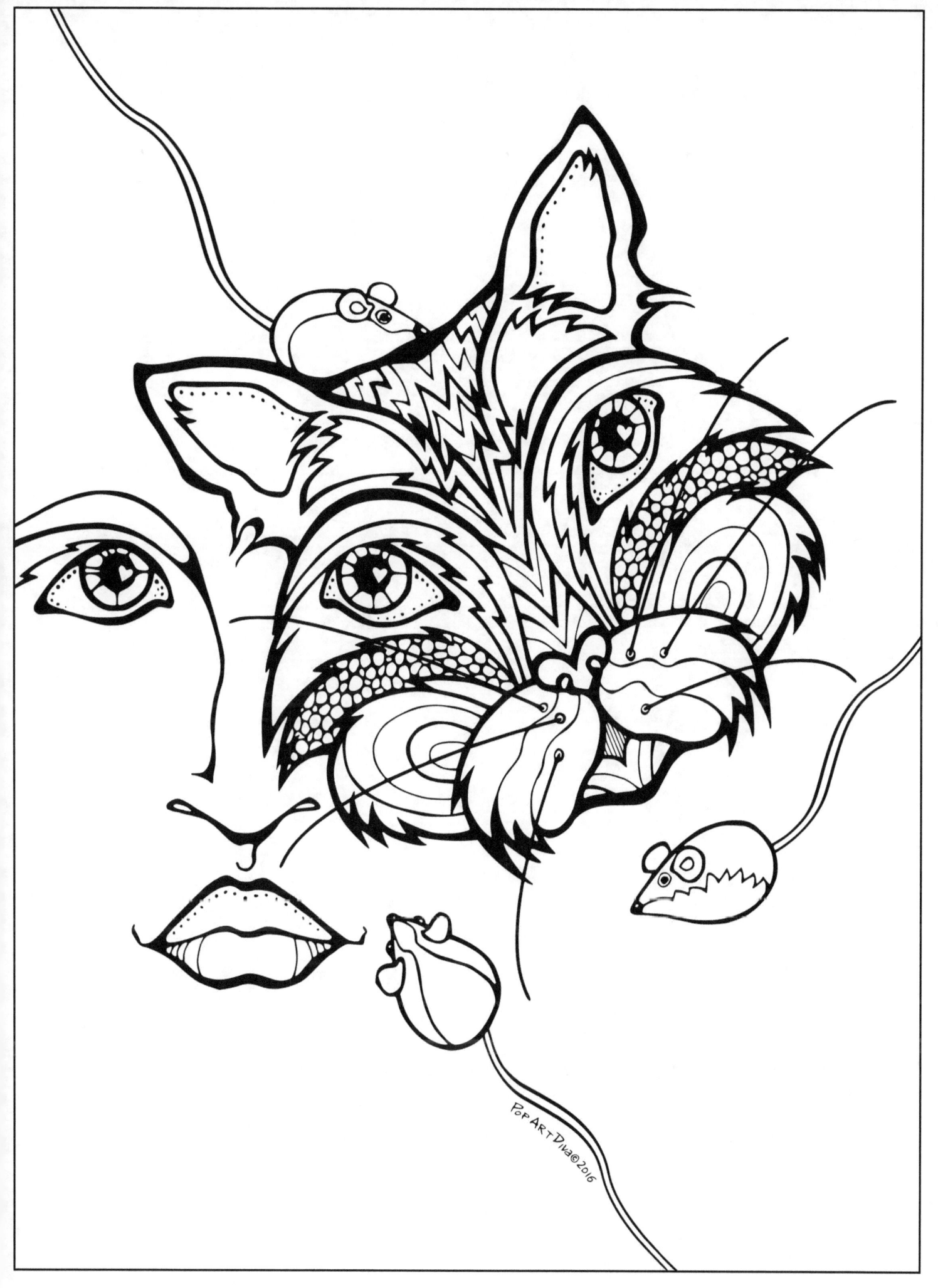

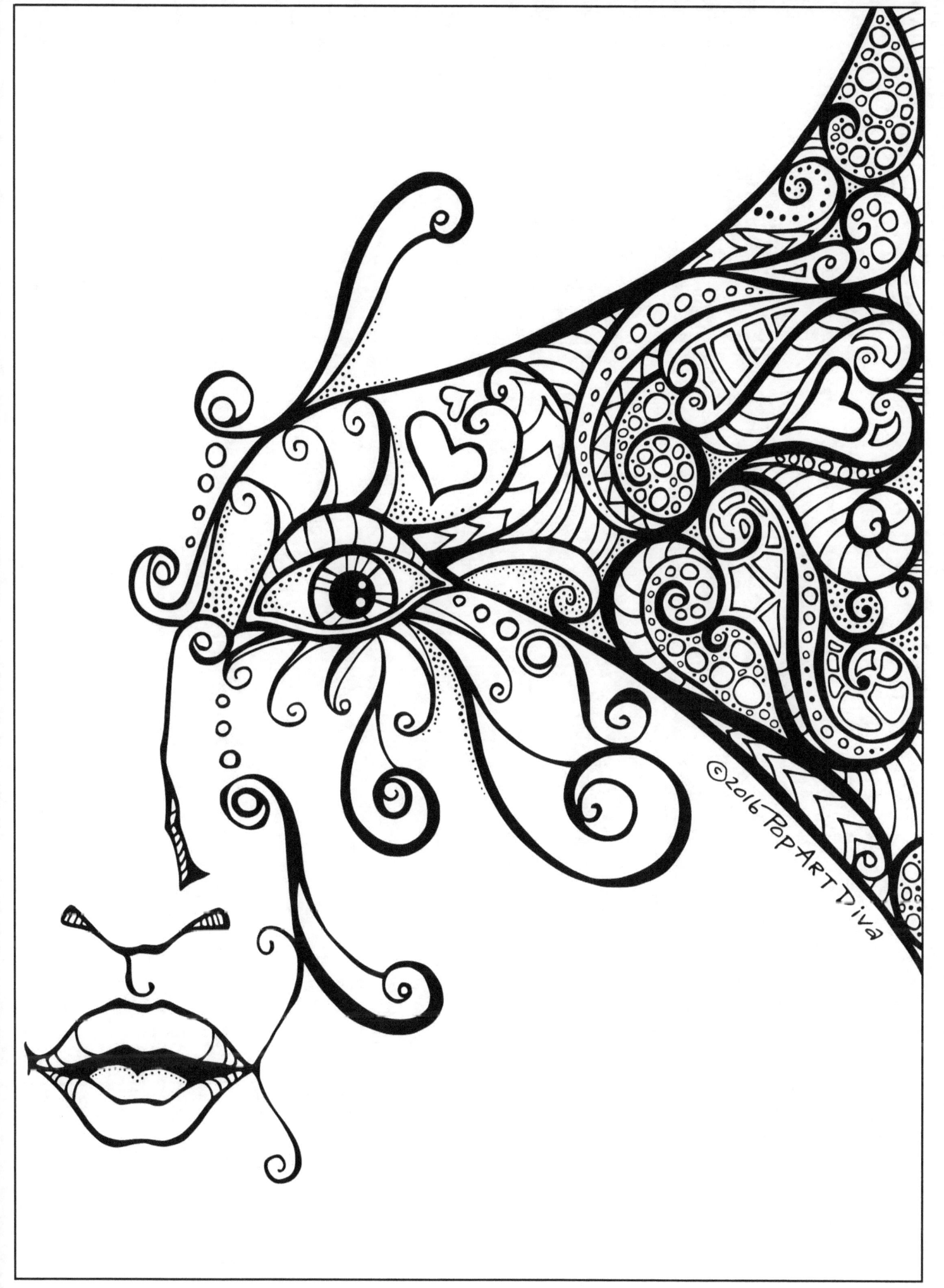

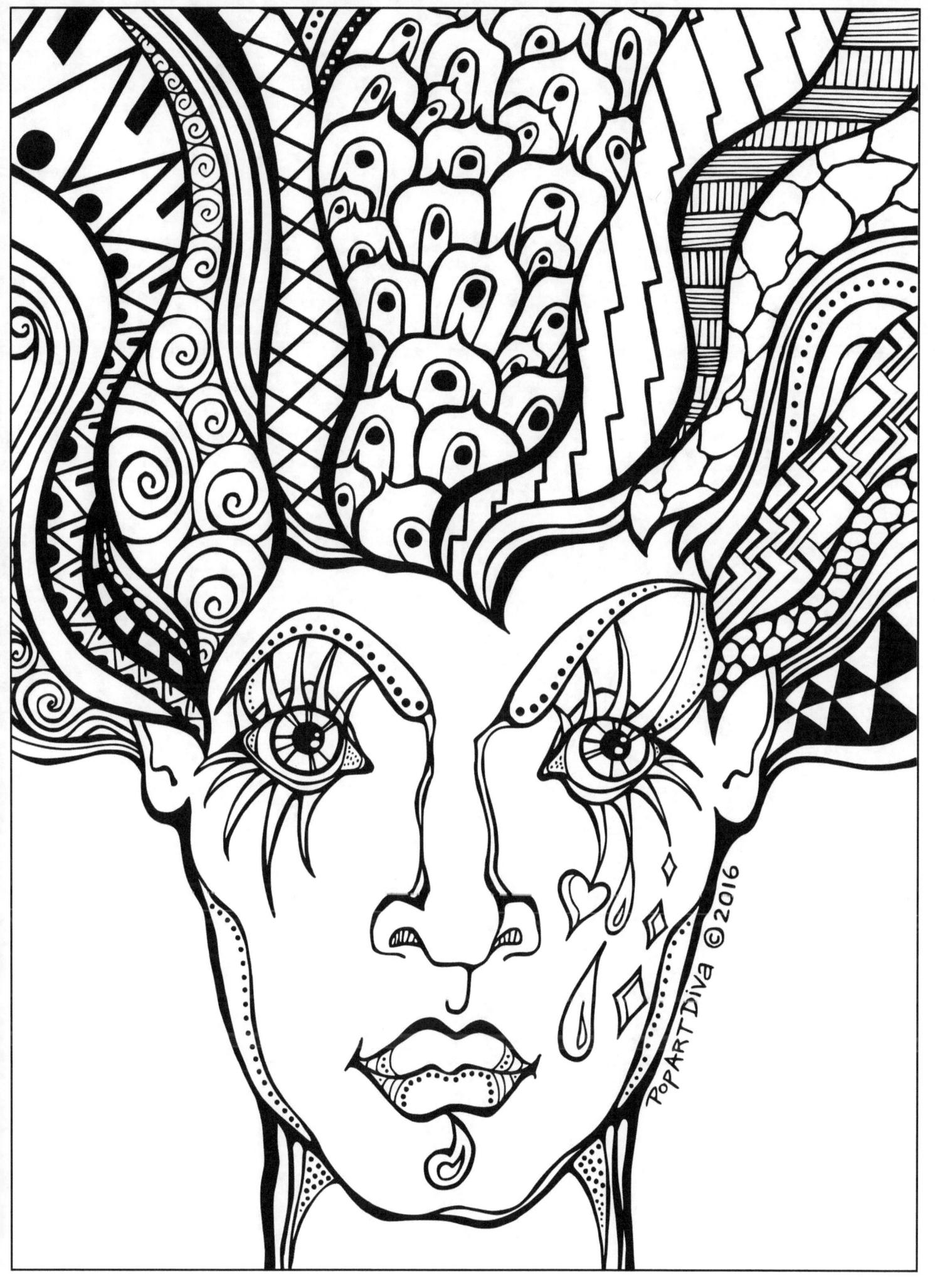

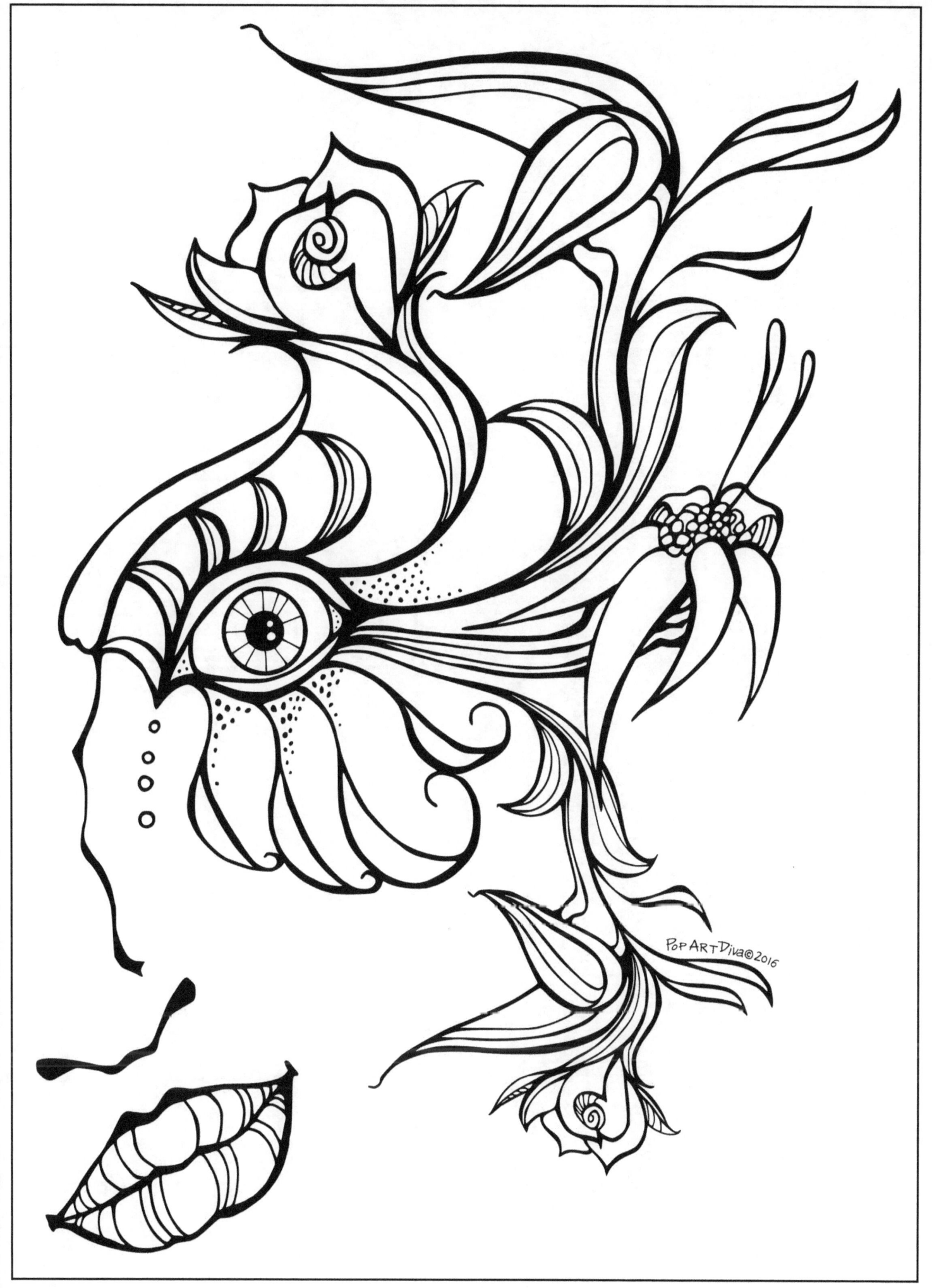

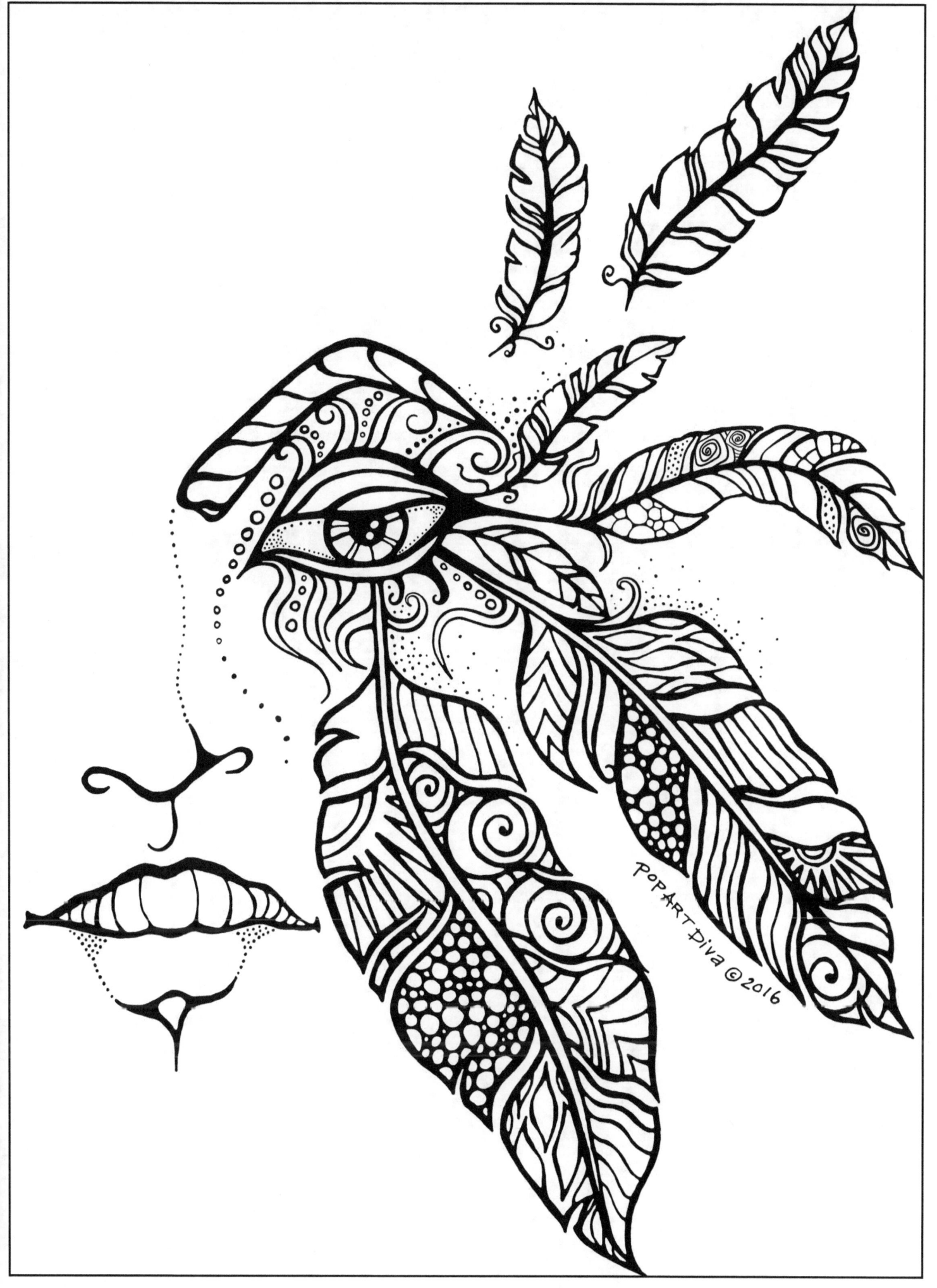

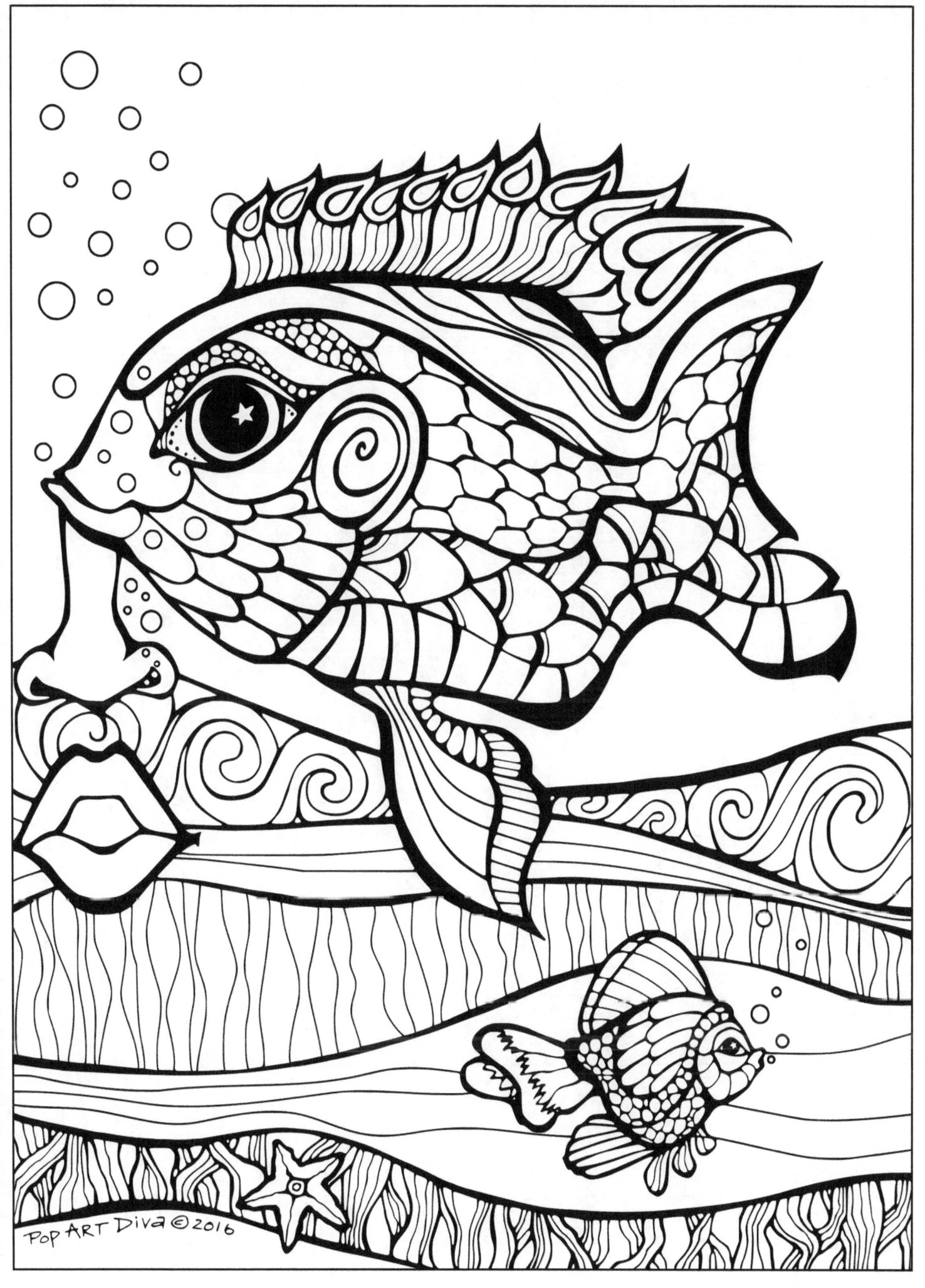

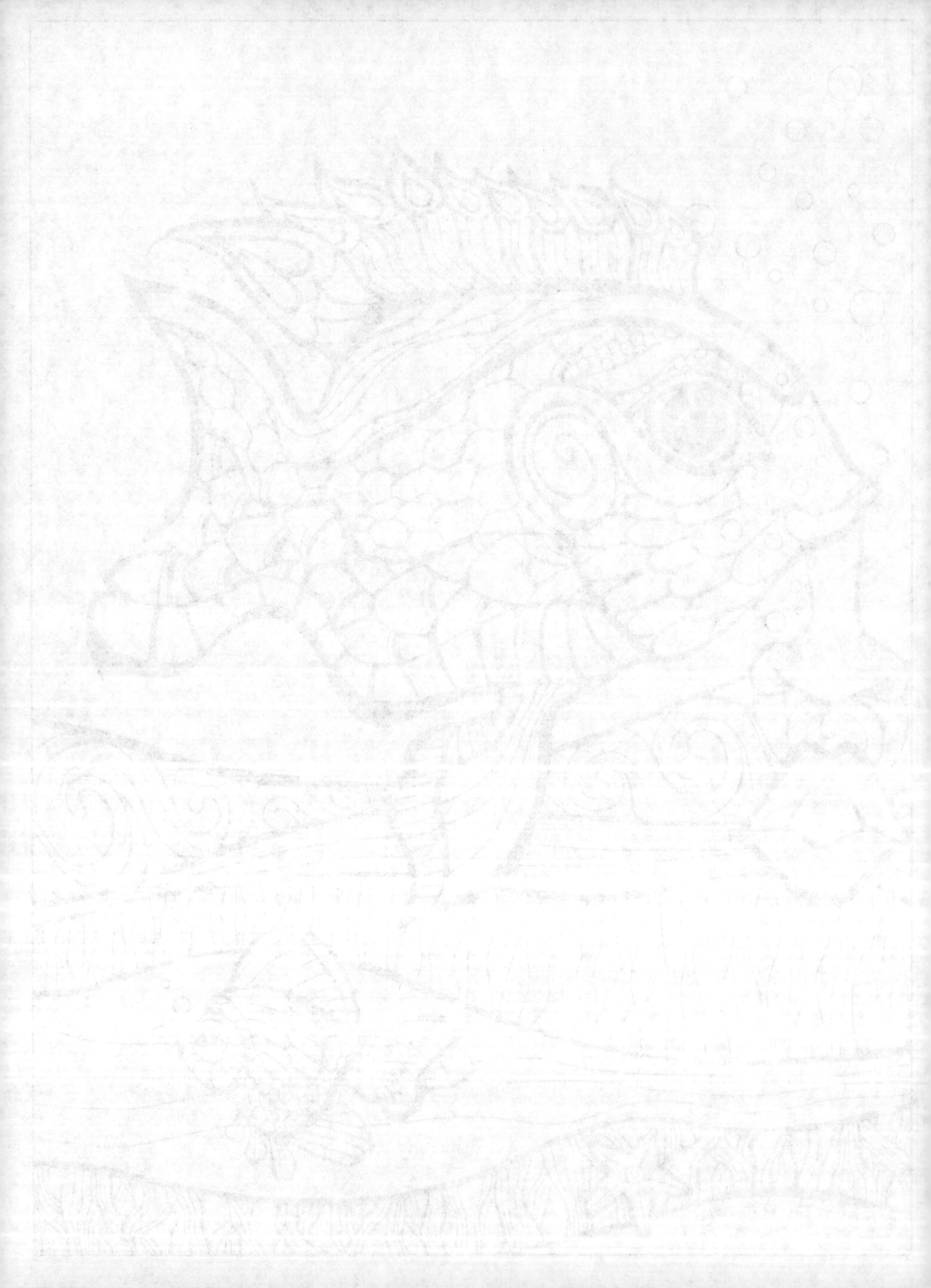

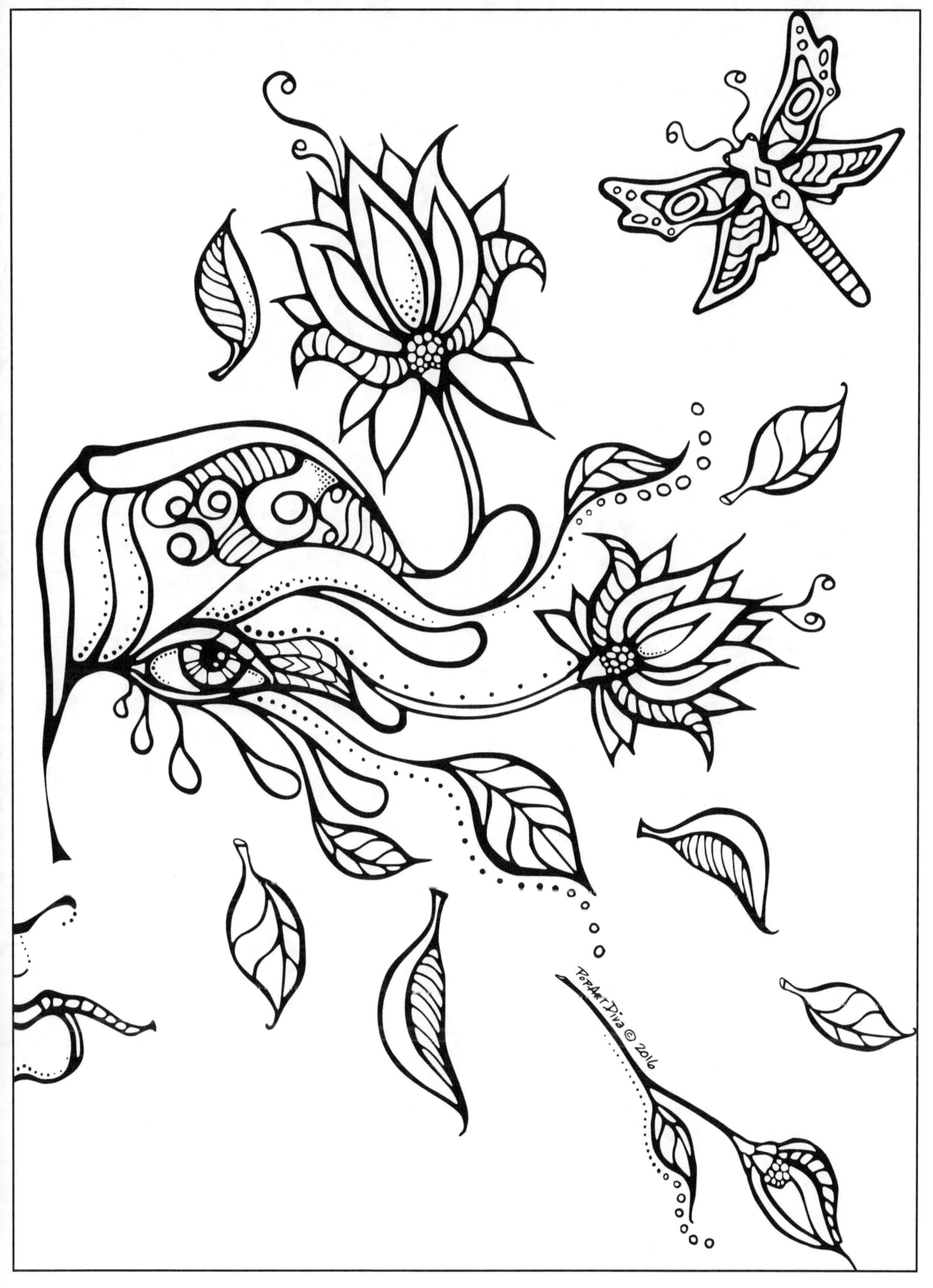

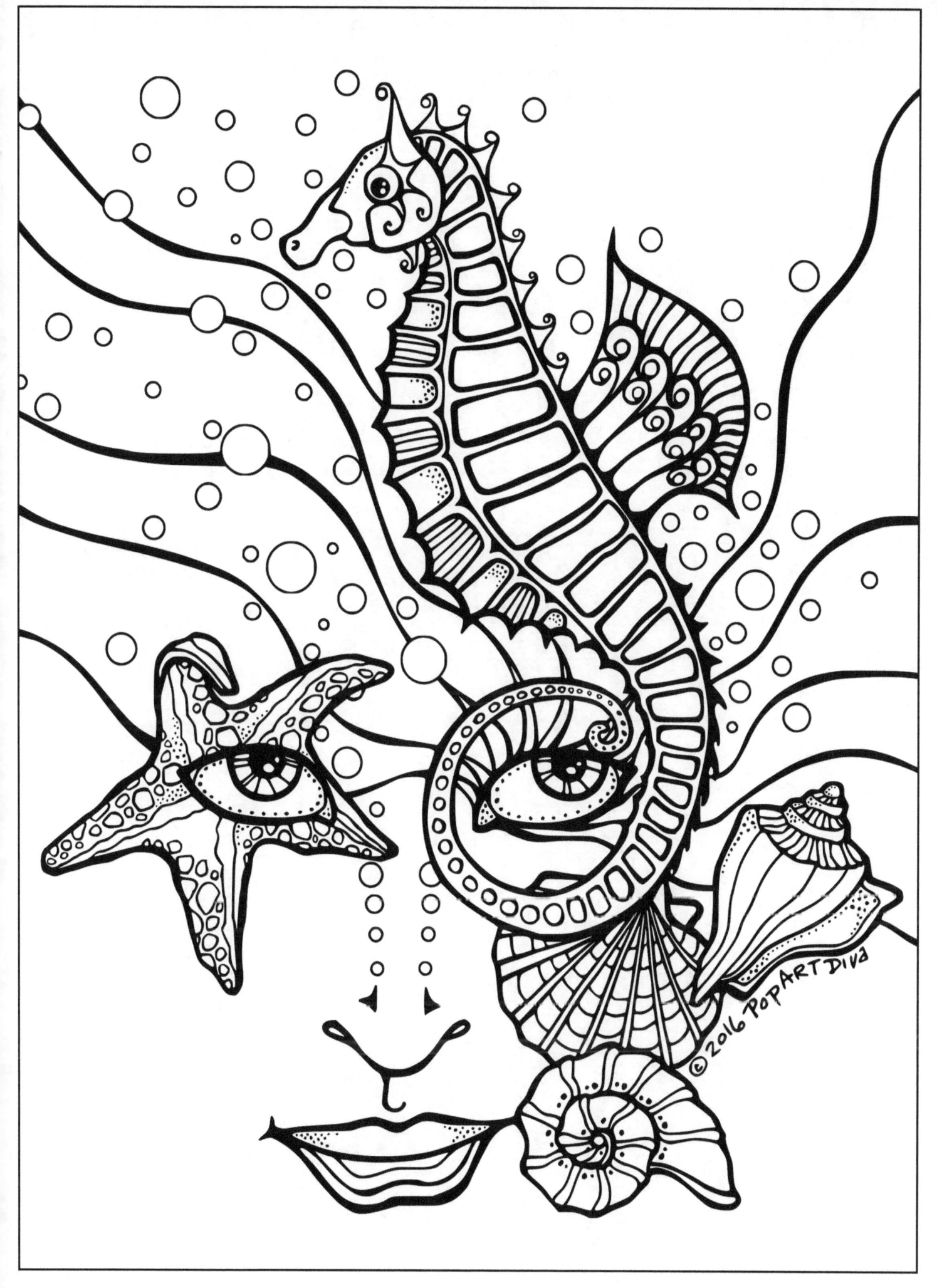

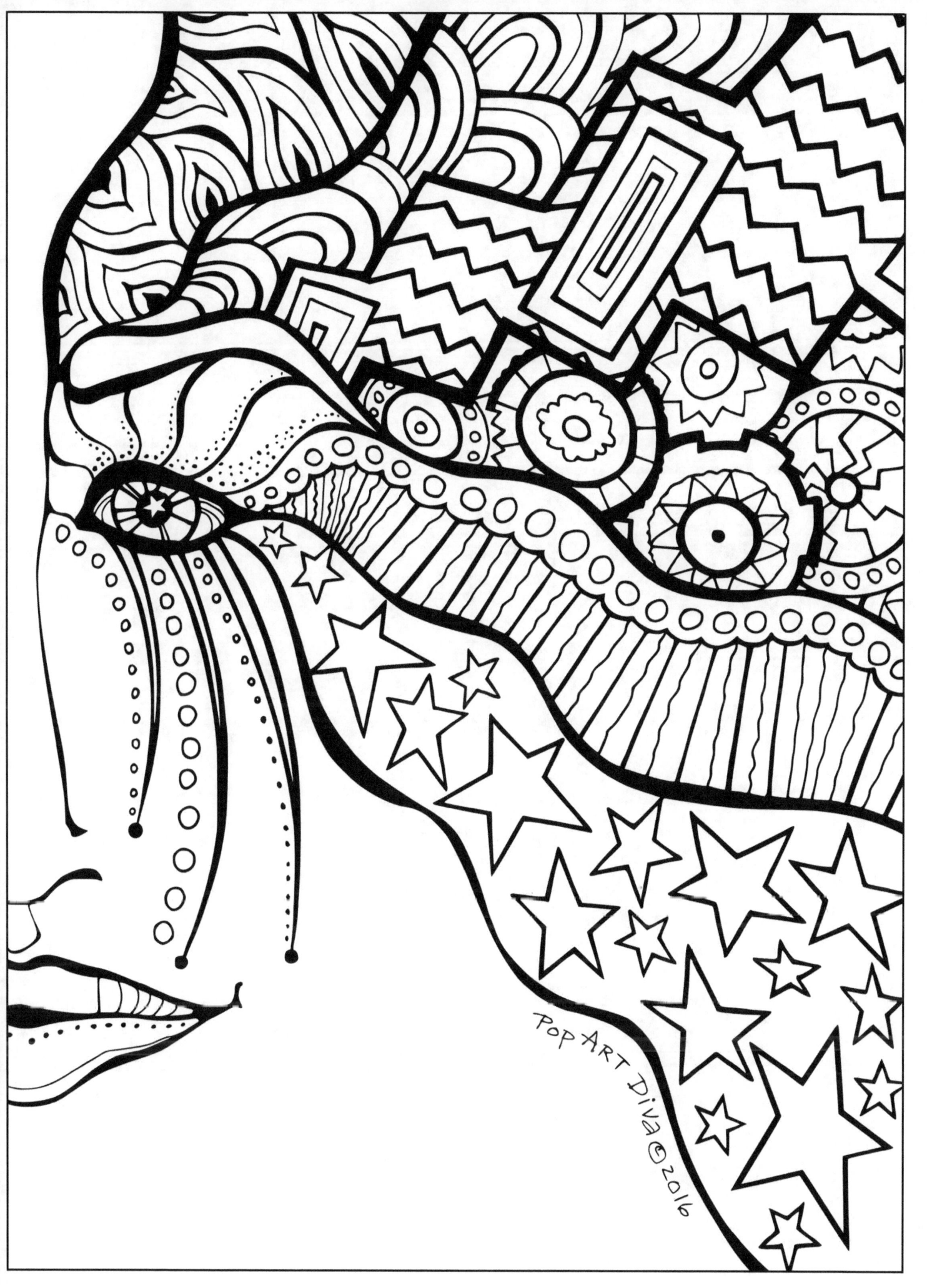

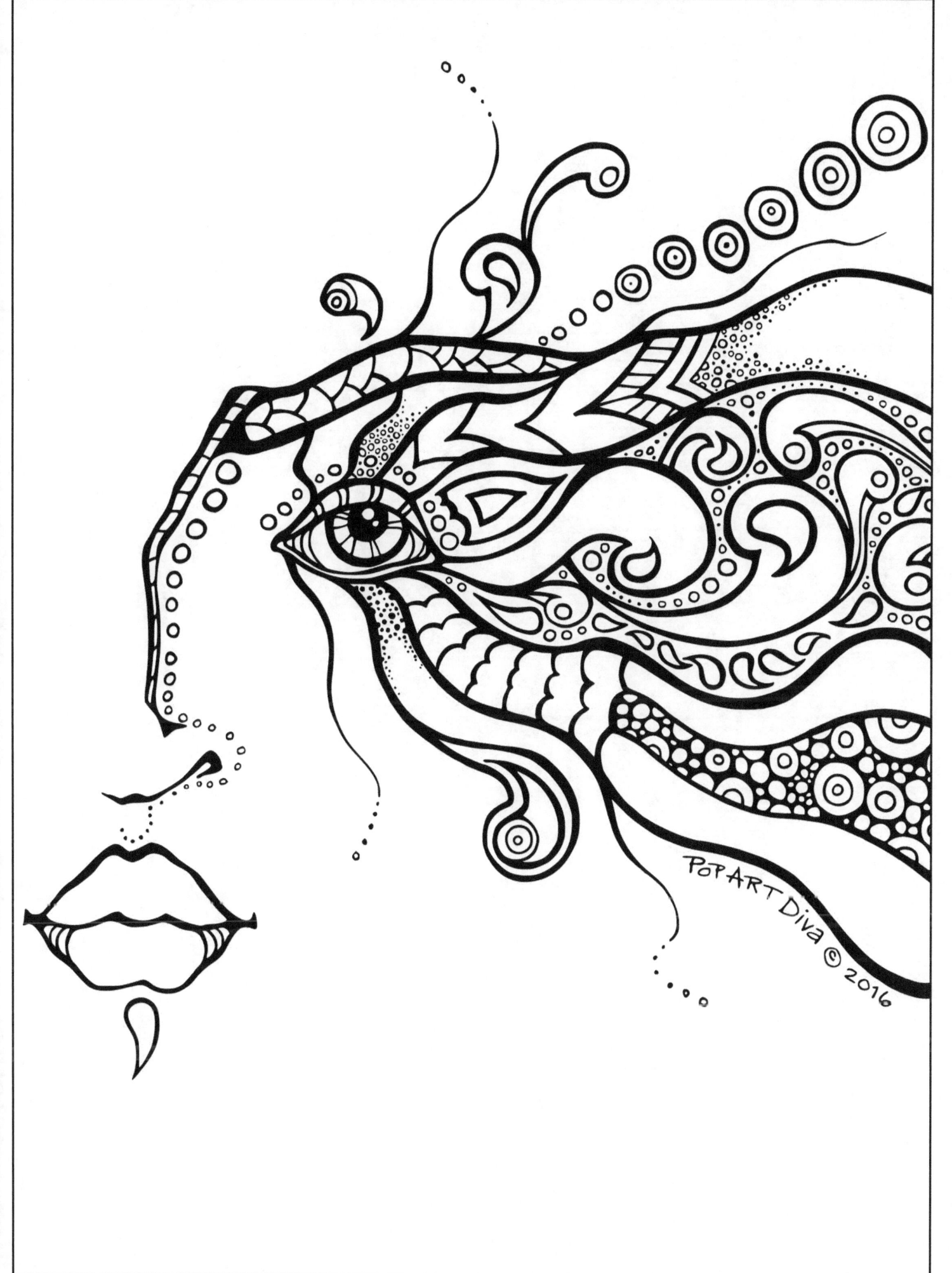

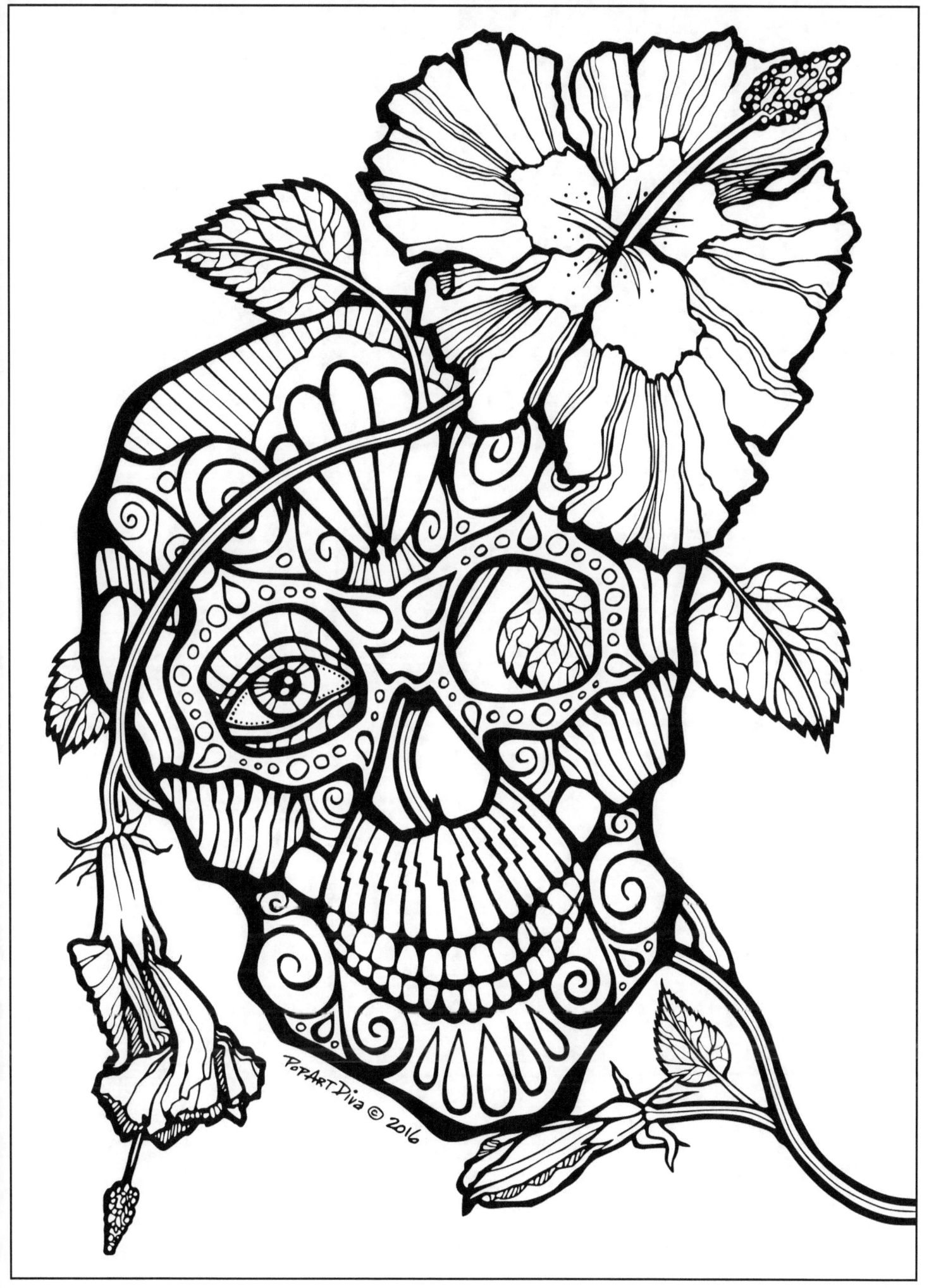

PopArtDiva © 2016

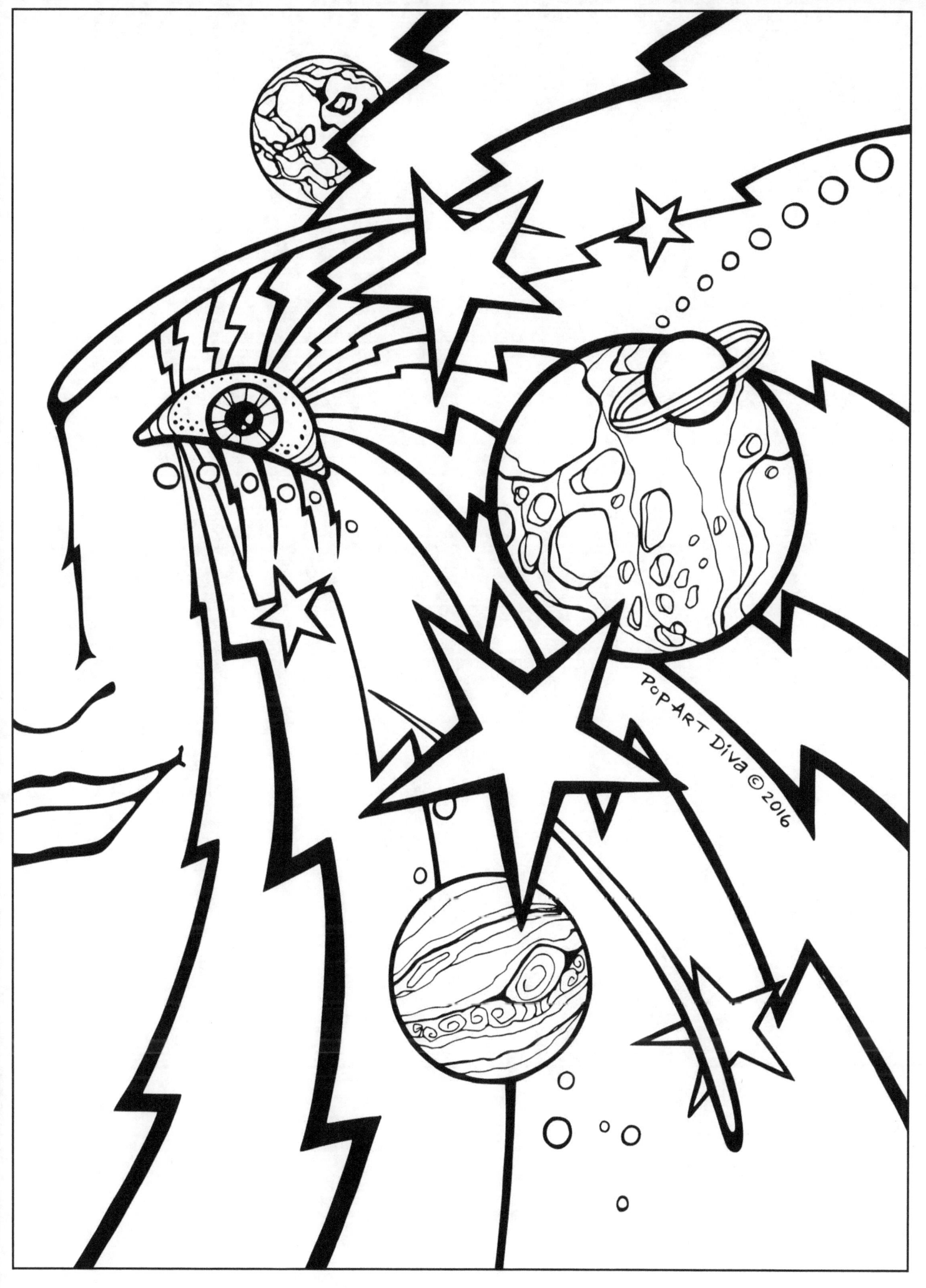

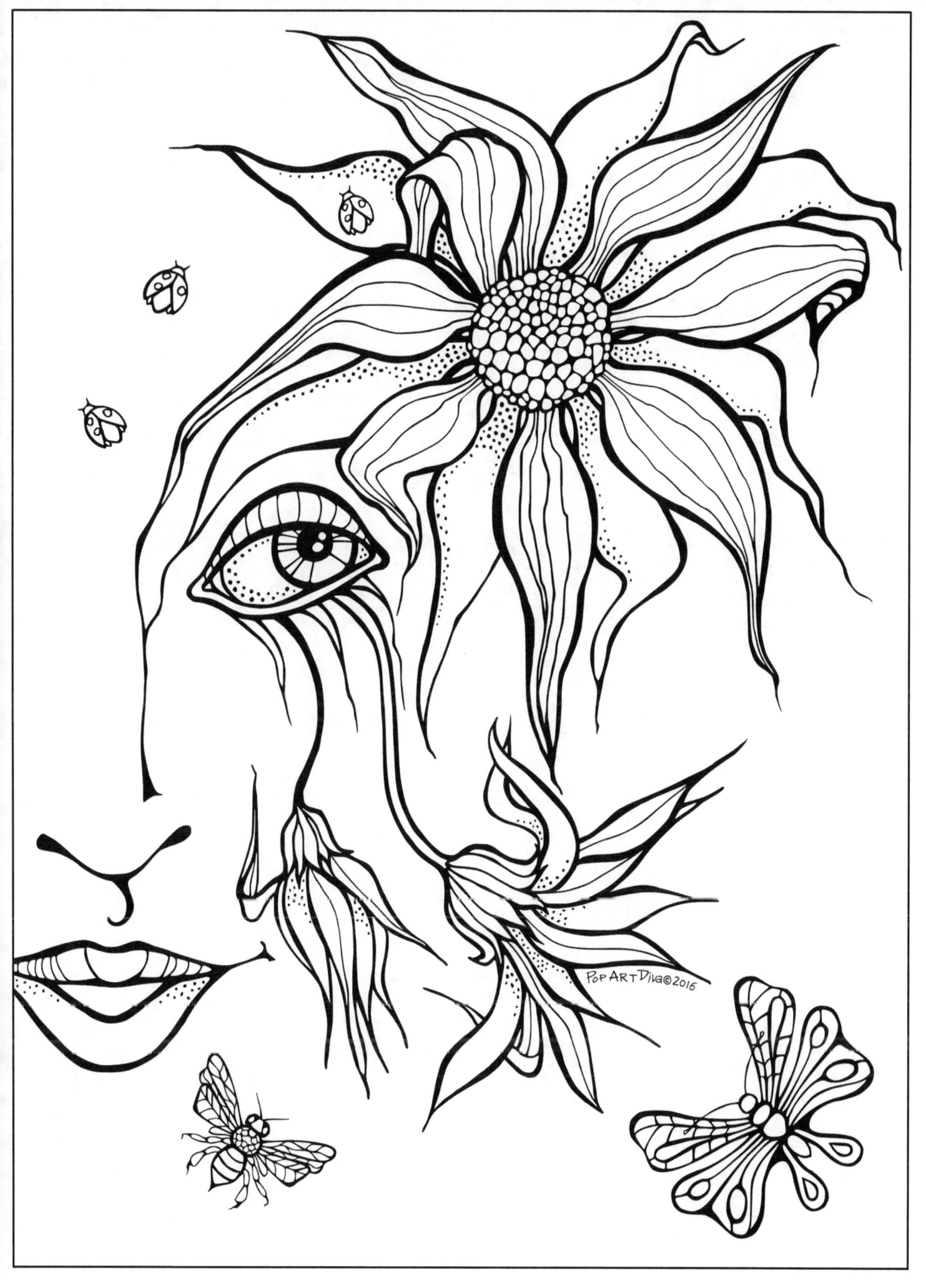

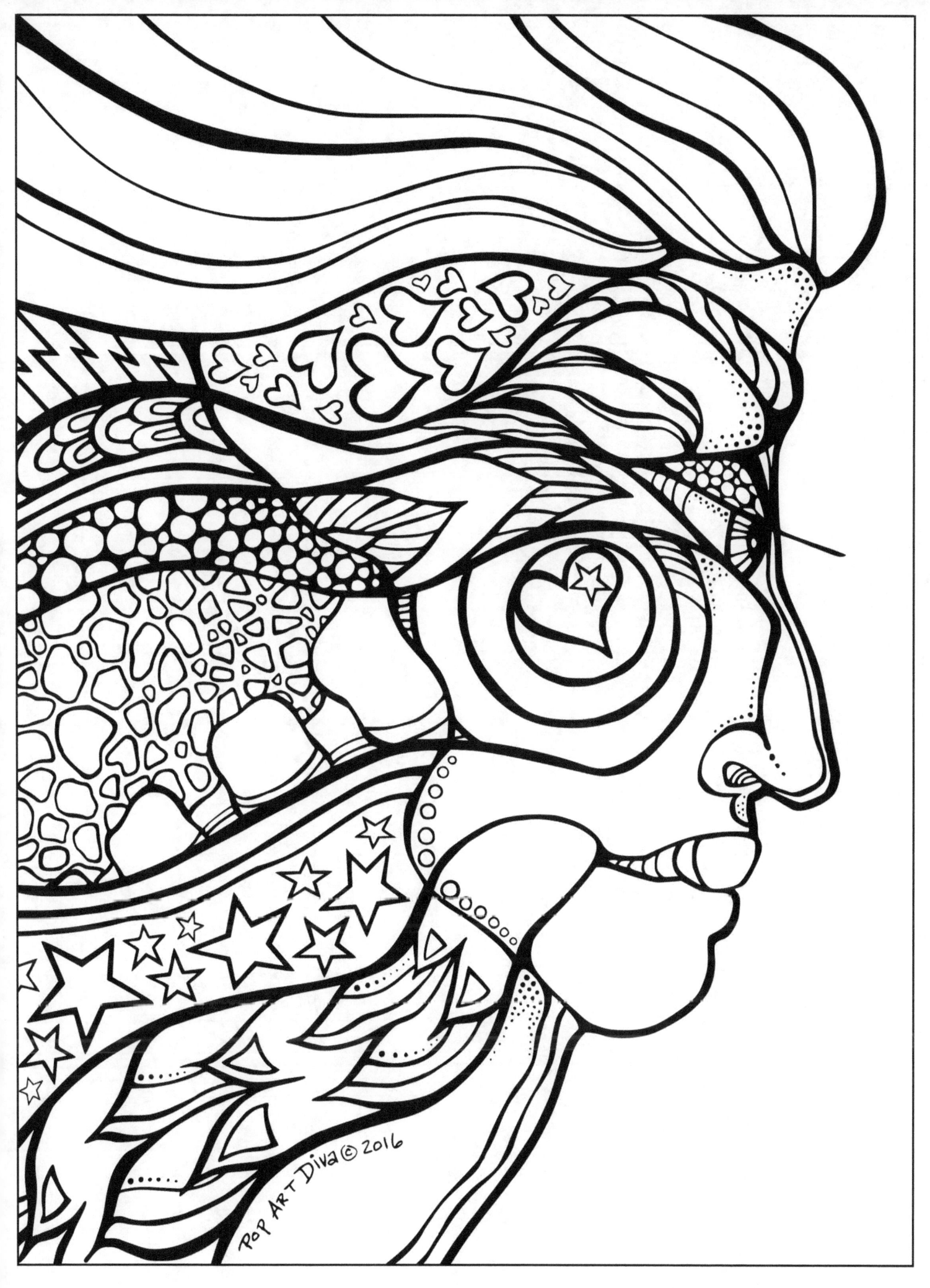

POP Art Diva © 2016

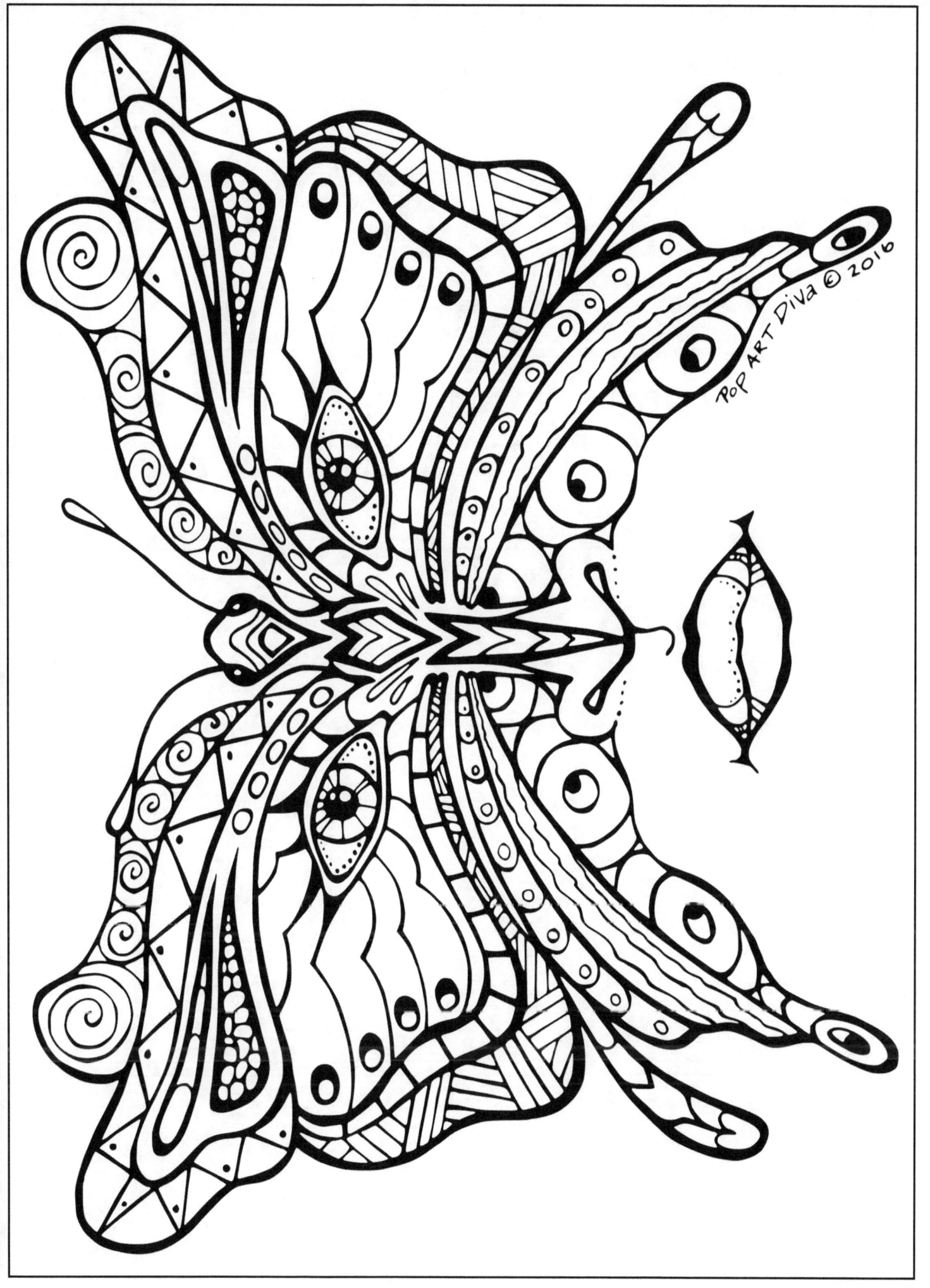

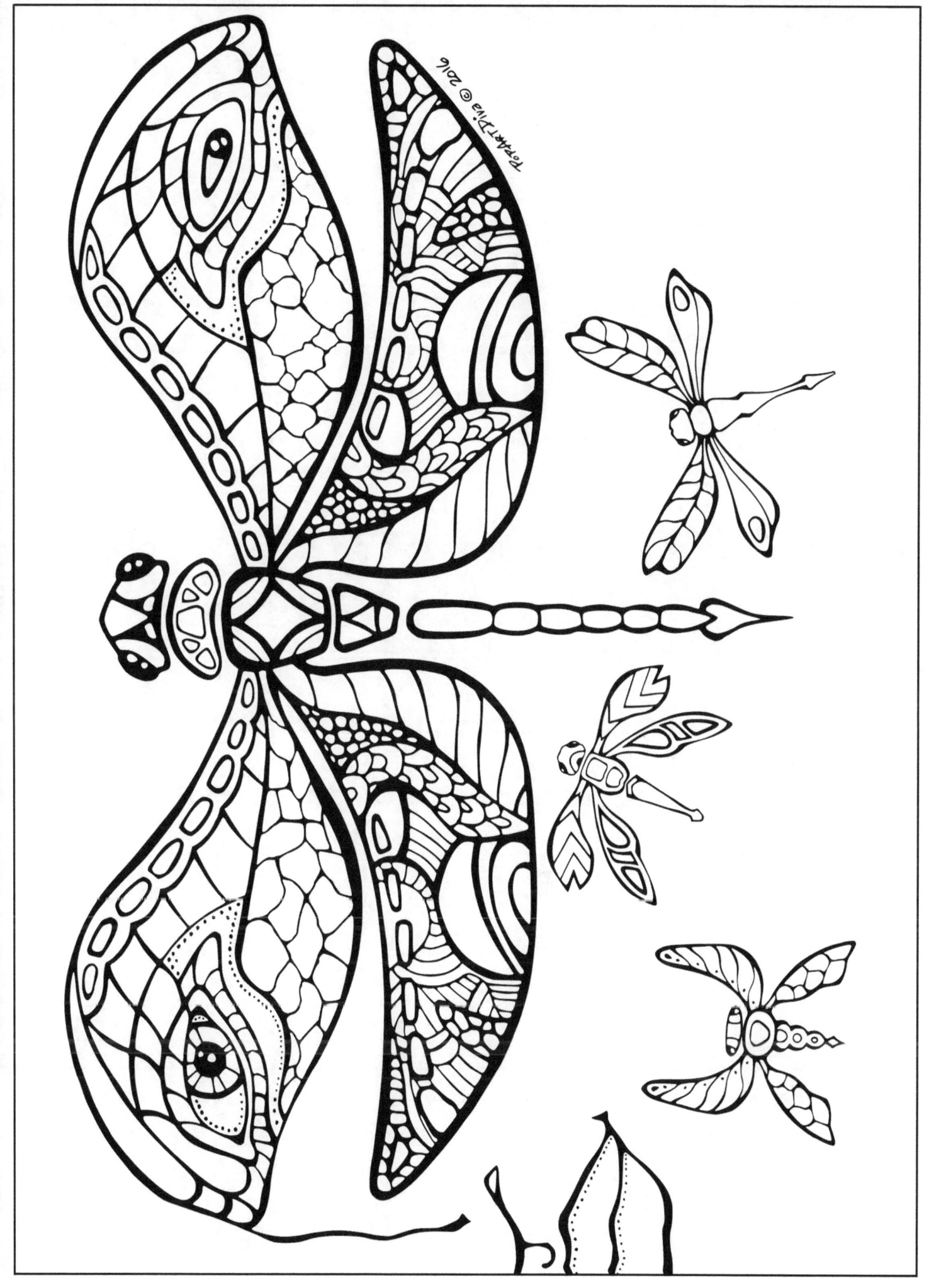

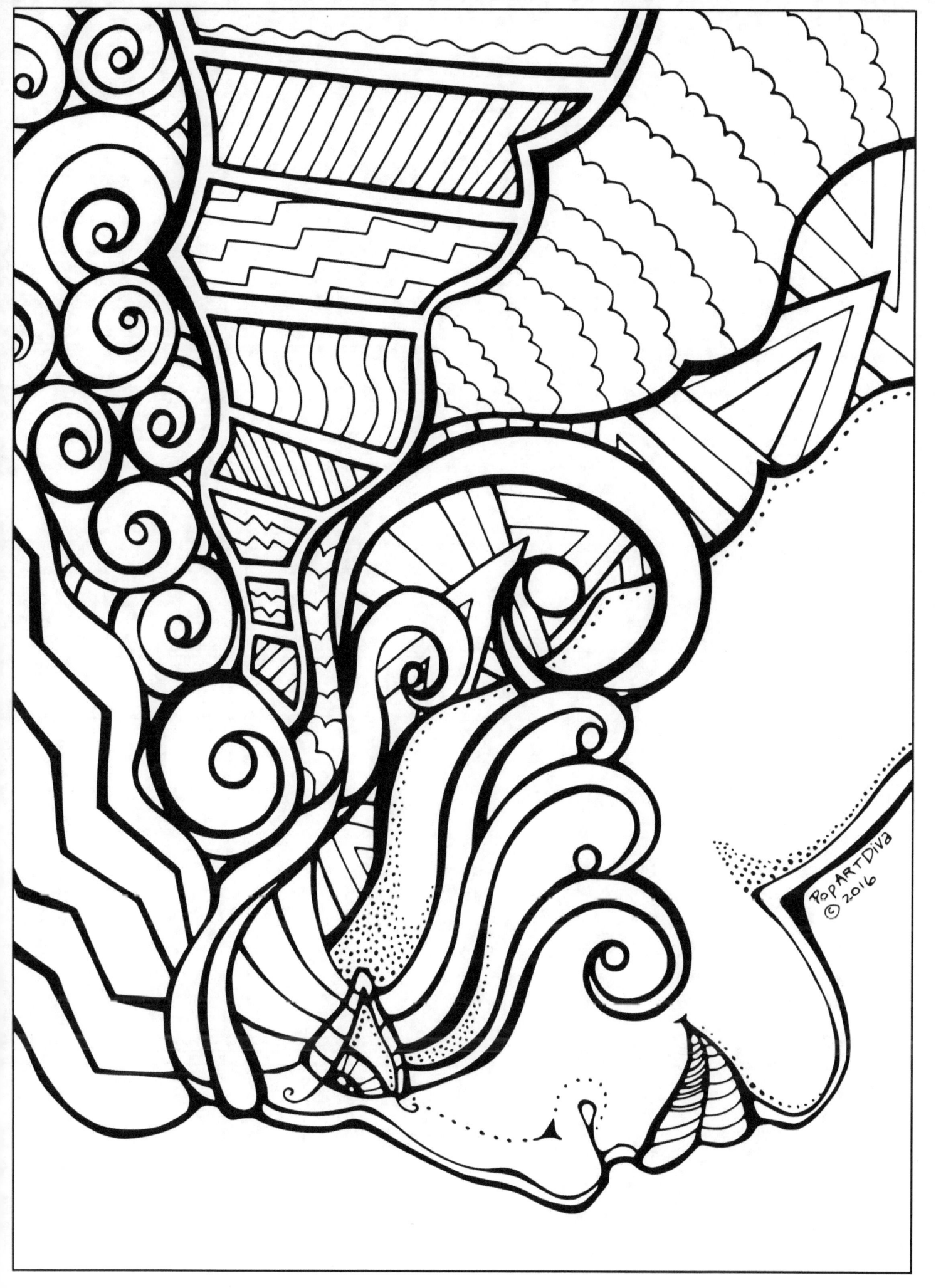

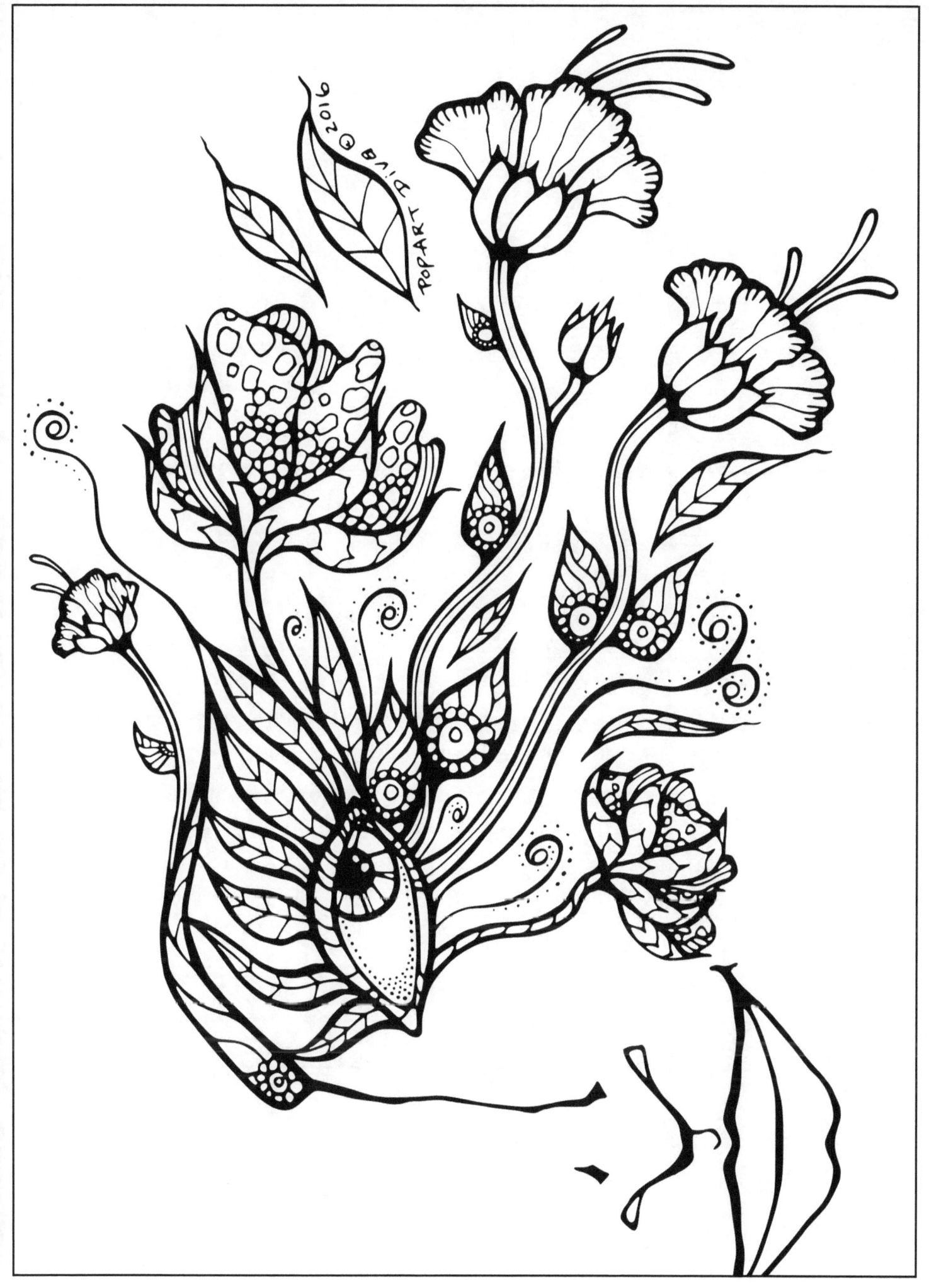

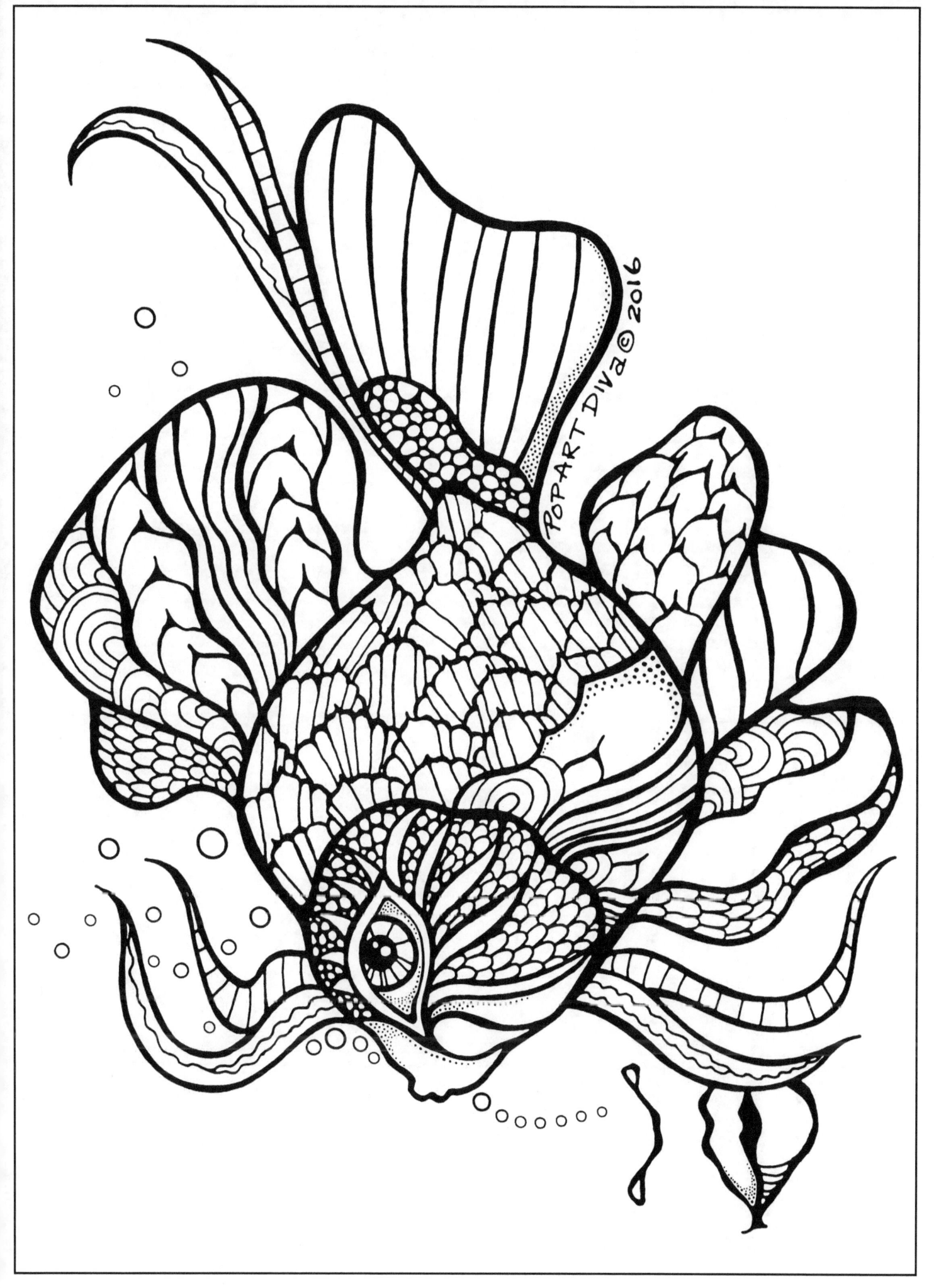

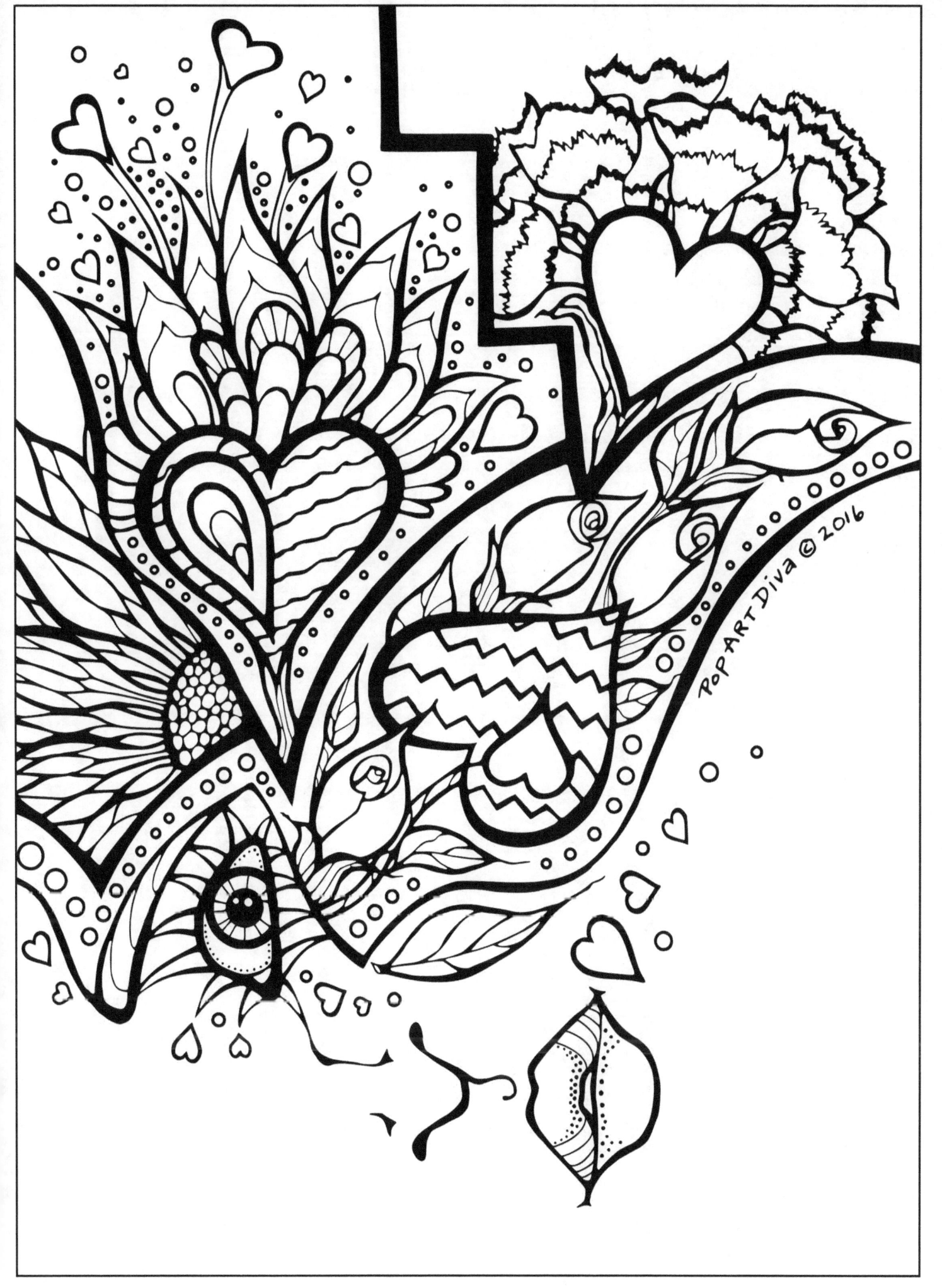

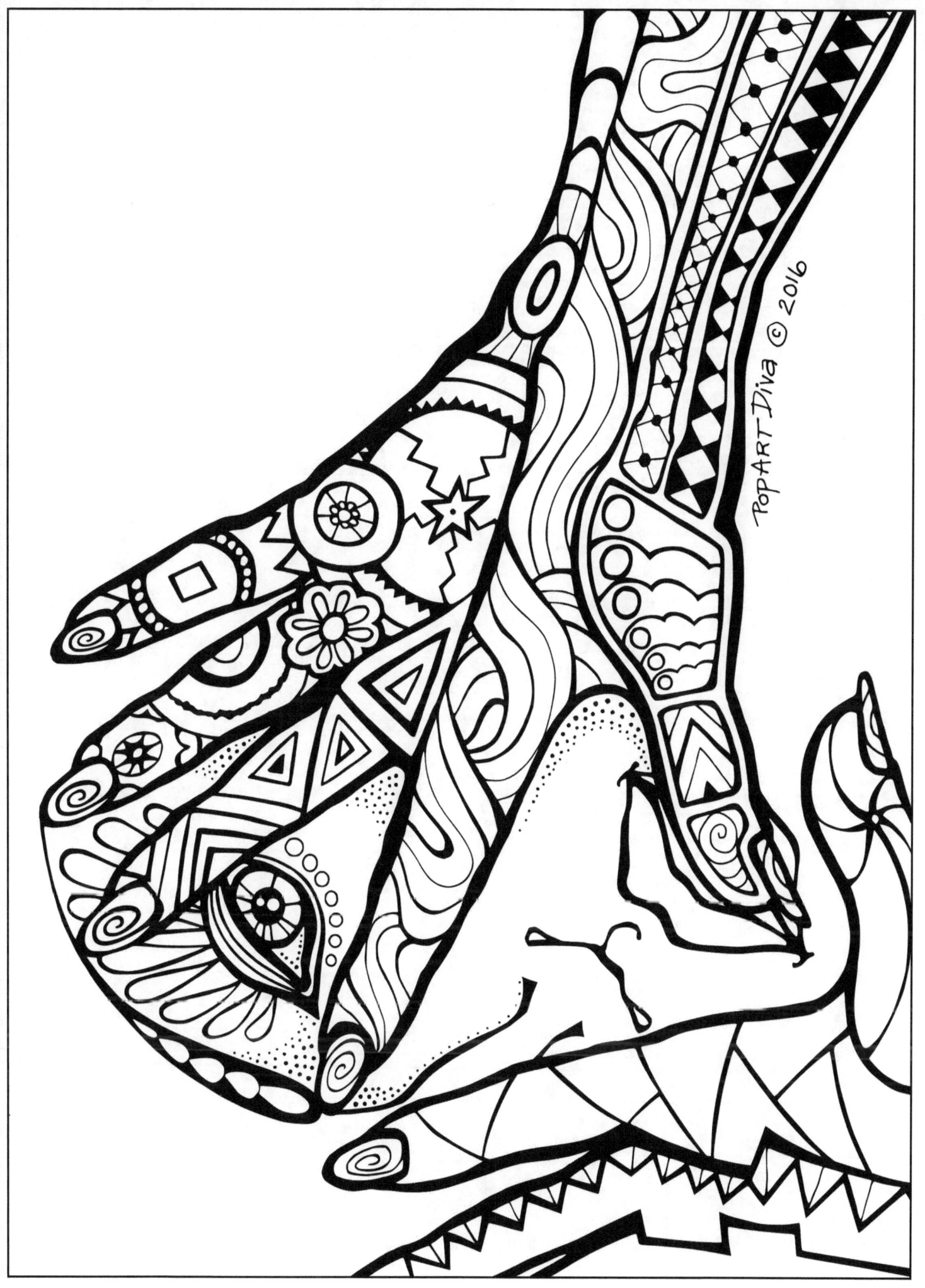

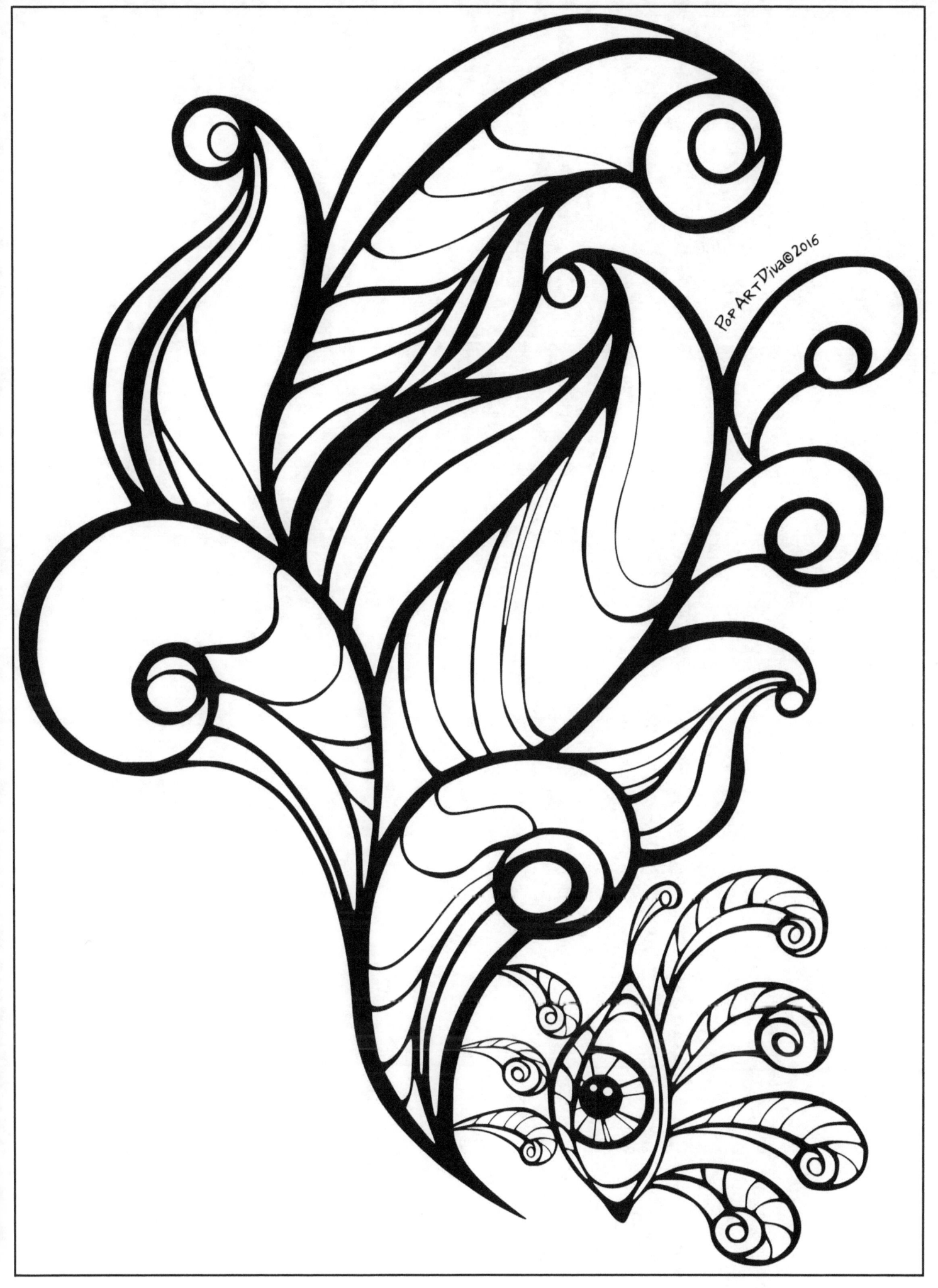

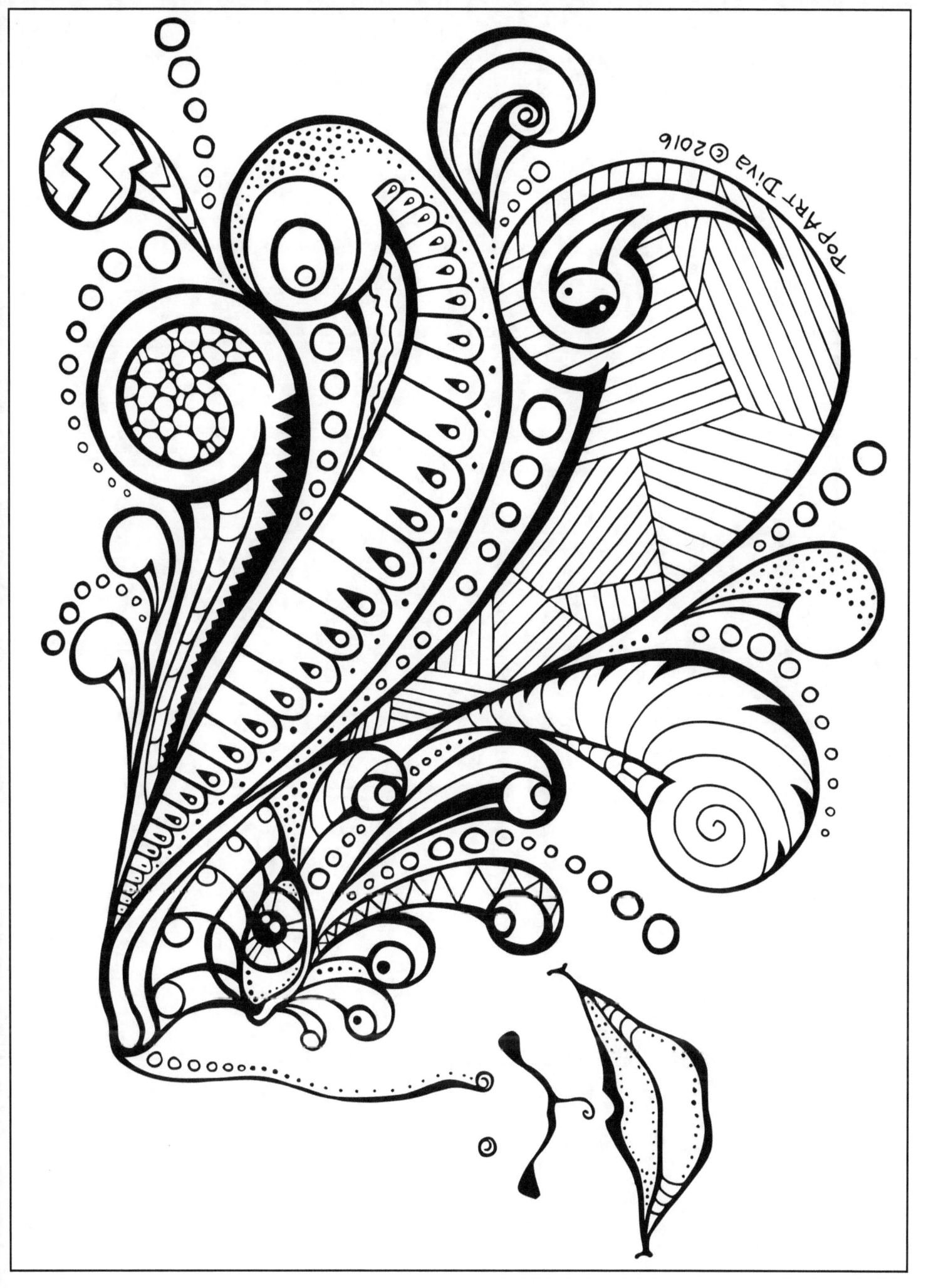

PopArt Diva © 2016

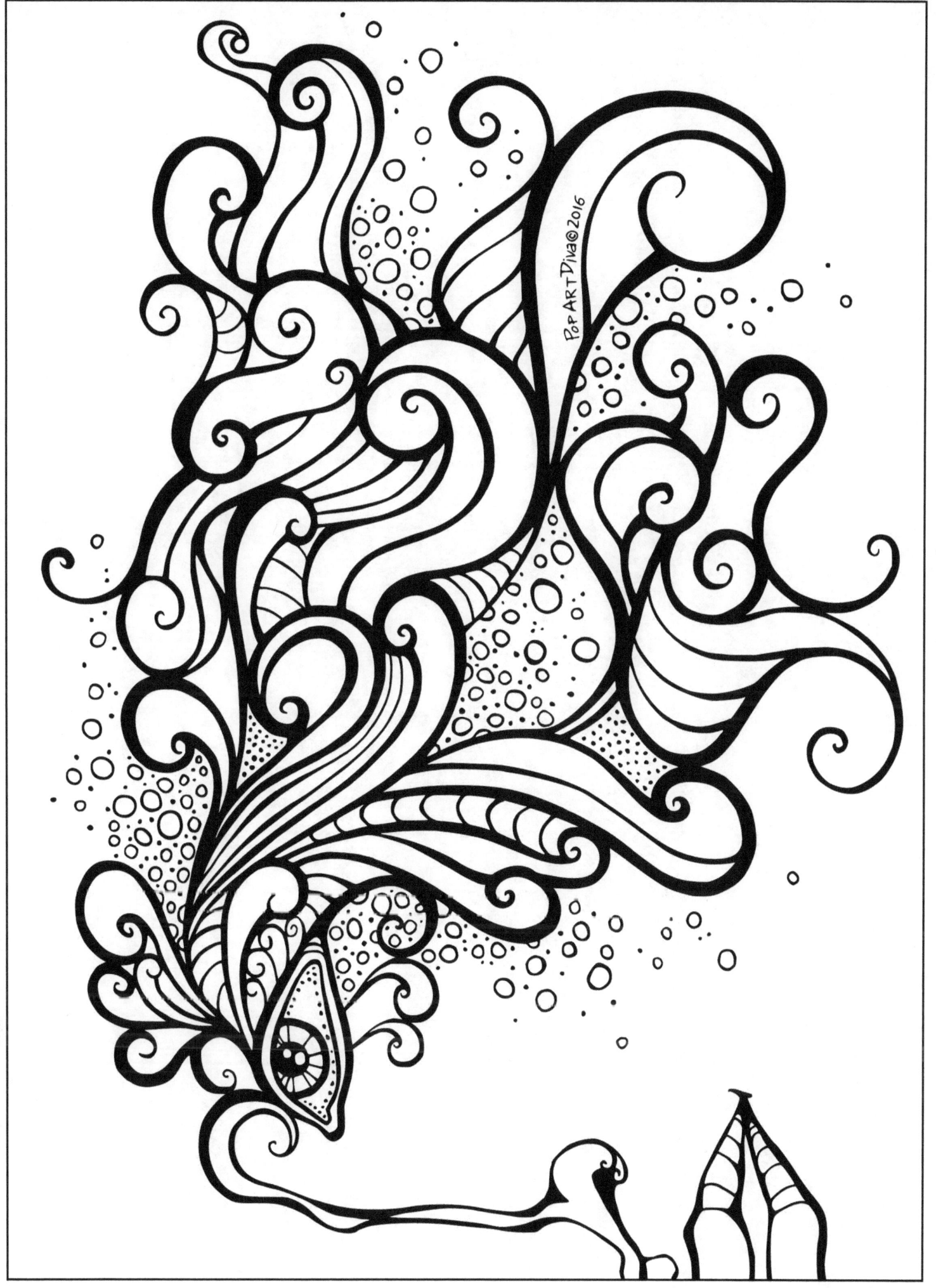

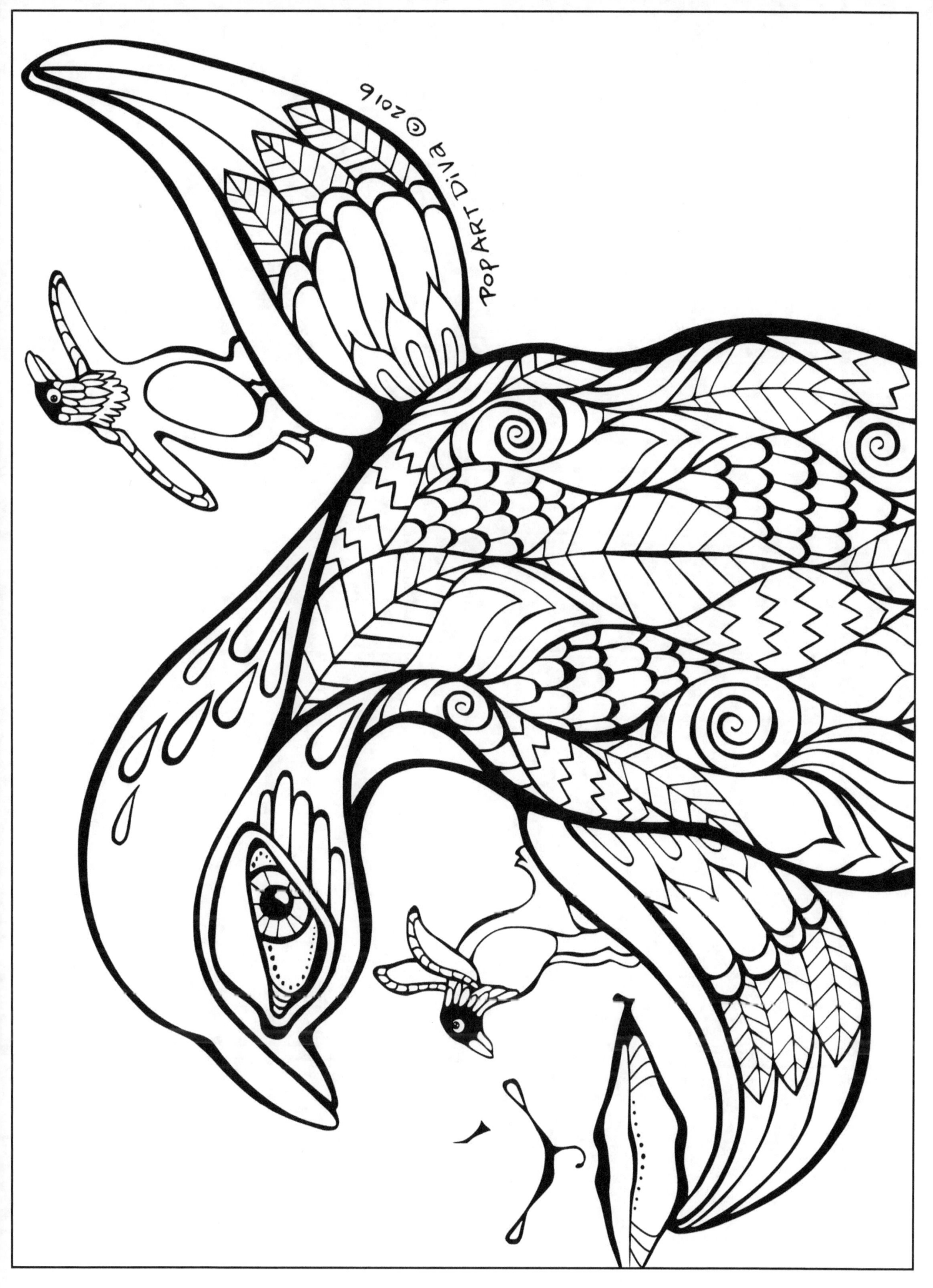

PopART DiVa © 2016

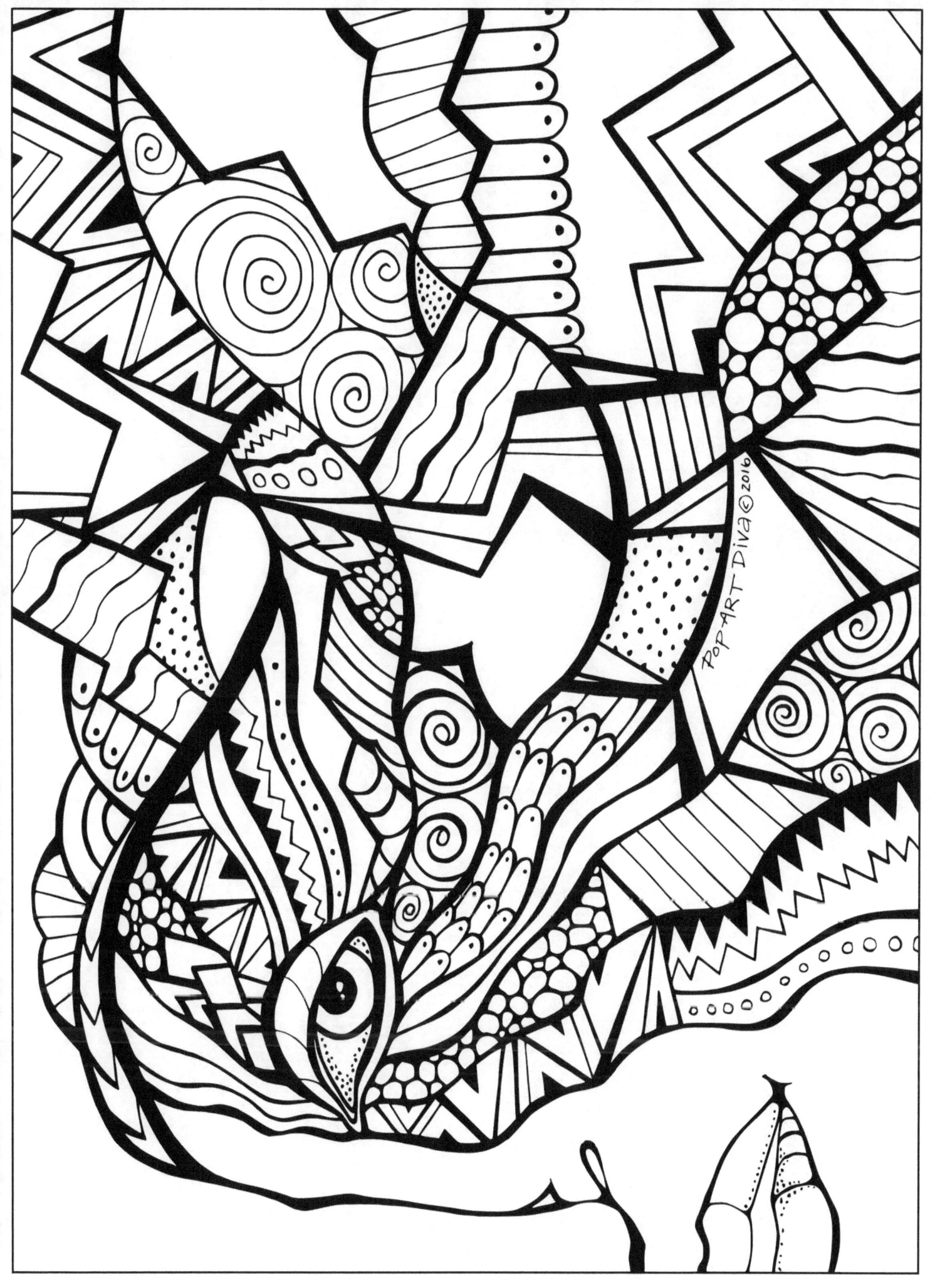

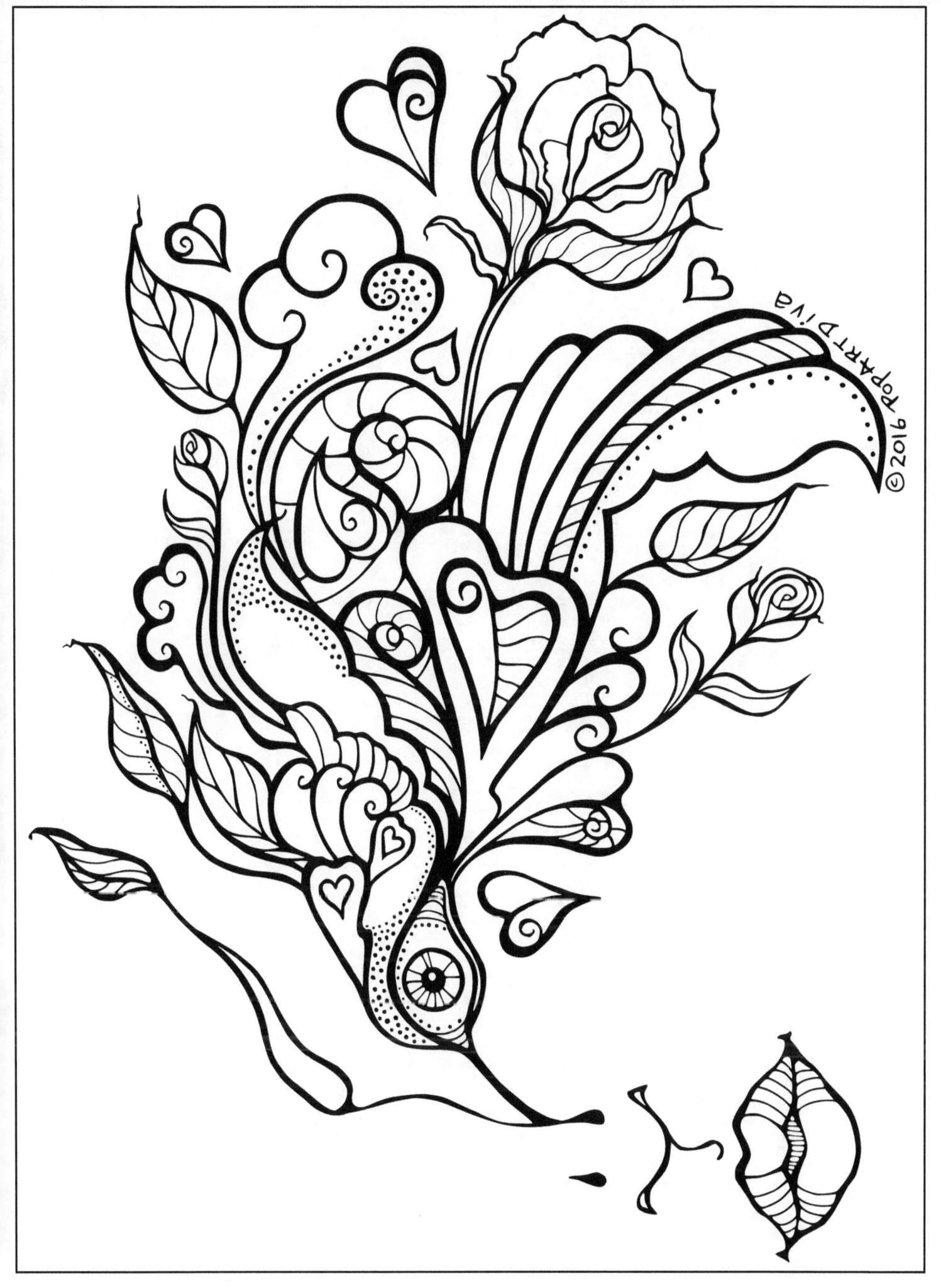

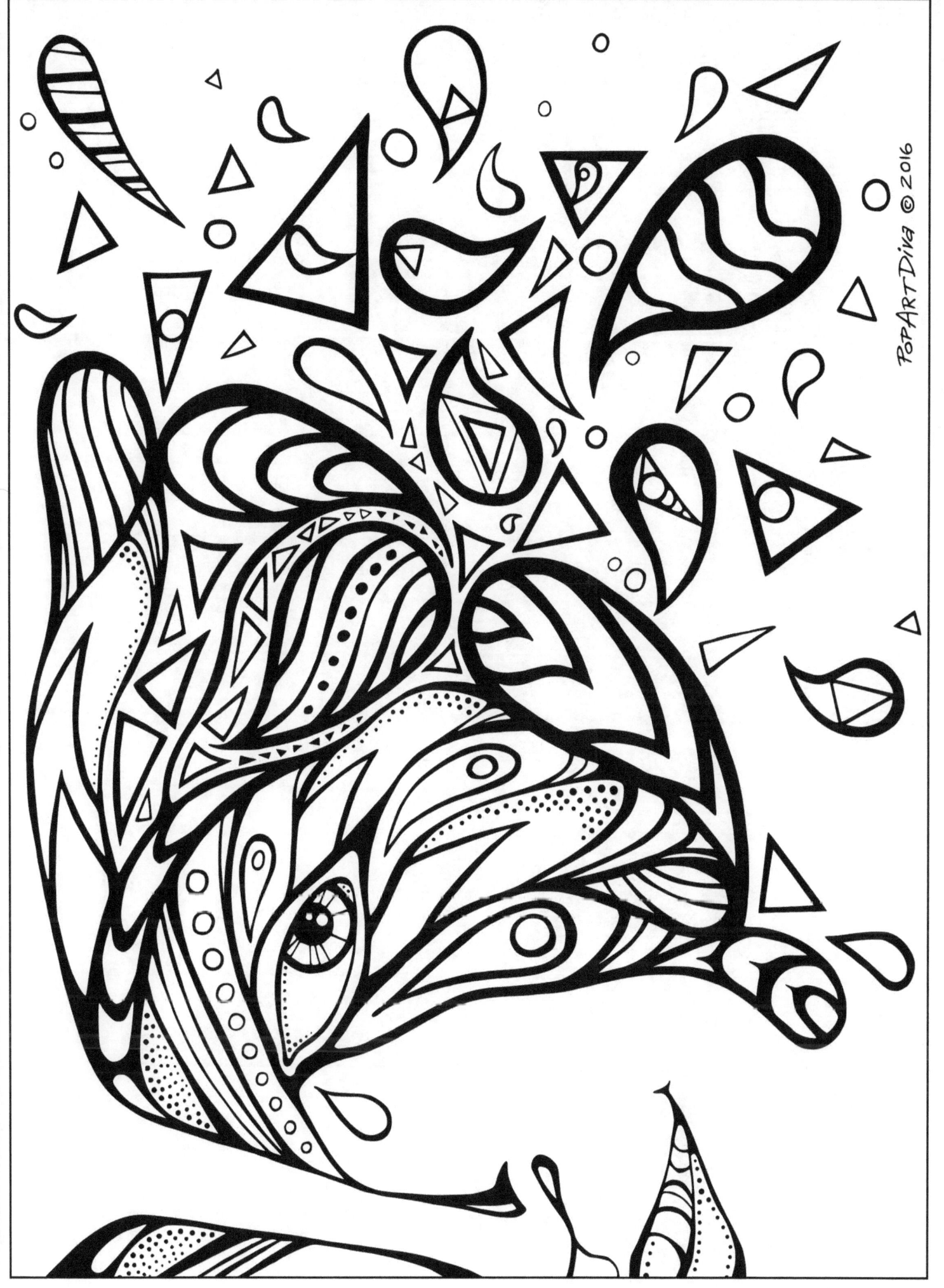

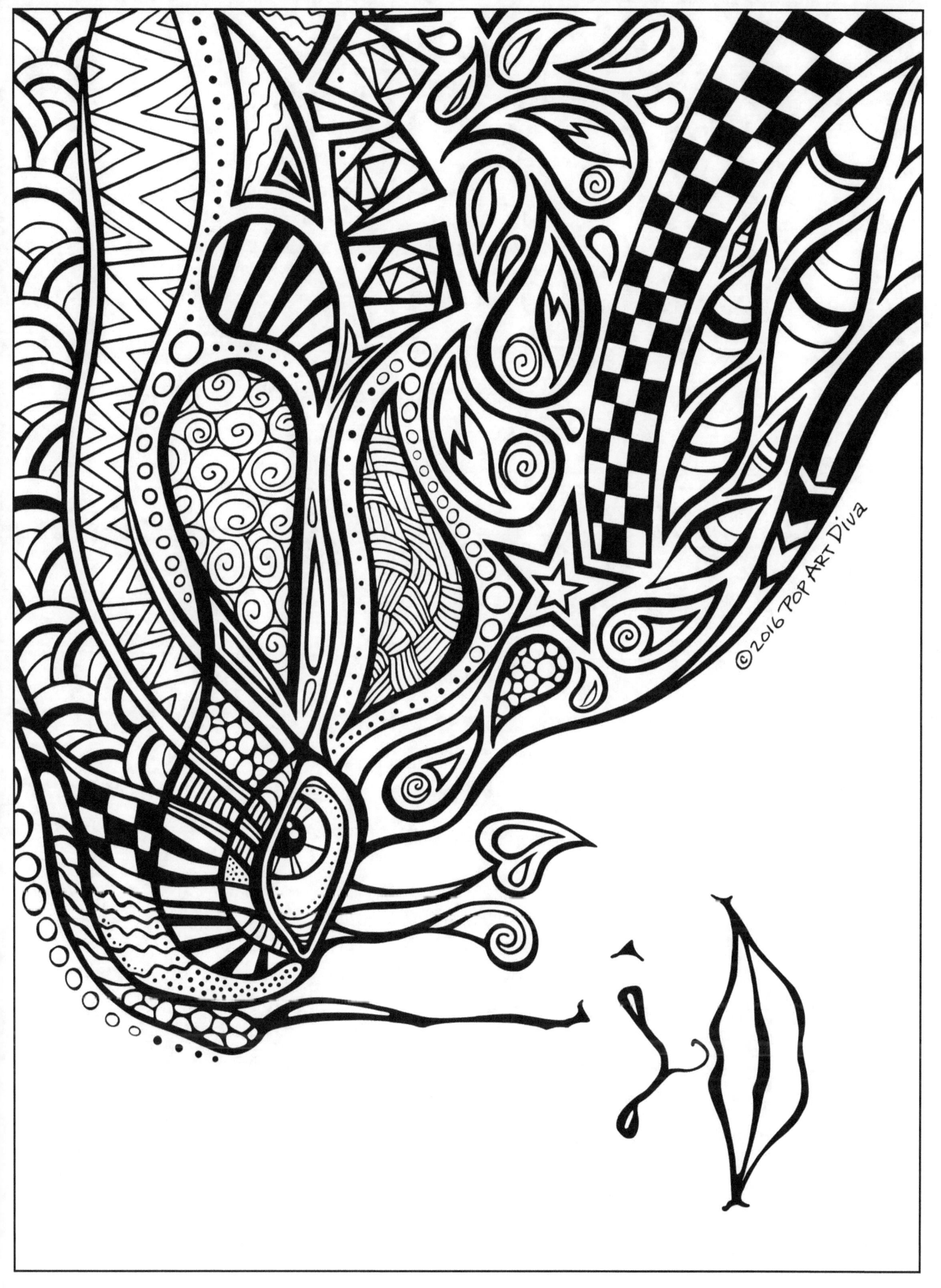

©2016 Pop Art Diva

TEST PAGE
Check your colors, test for bleed through, try out color palettes on these pages!

TEST PAGE

TEST PAGE

TEST PAGE

TEST PAGE

TEST PAGE

TEST PAGE

COLORING MEDIUM TEST CHART

#/ColorName	Test Color Inside Crayon	#/ColorName	Test Color Inside Crayon

COLORING MEDIUM TEST CHART ©2016 by PopArtDiva, ColoringLifeHappy.Com

| #/ColorName | Test Color Inside Crayon | #/ColorName | Test Color Inside Crayon |

COLORING MEDIUM TEST CHART ©2016 by PopArtDiva, ColoringLifeHappy.Com

#/ColorName	Test Color Inside Crayon	#/ColorName	Test Color Inside Crayon
_____		_____	
_____		_____	
_____		_____	
_____		_____	
_____		_____	
_____		_____	
_____		_____	
_____		_____	
_____		_____	
_____		_____	
_____		_____	
_____		_____	
_____		_____	
_____		_____	
_____		_____	
_____		_____	
_____		_____	
_____		_____	
_____		_____	
_____		_____	

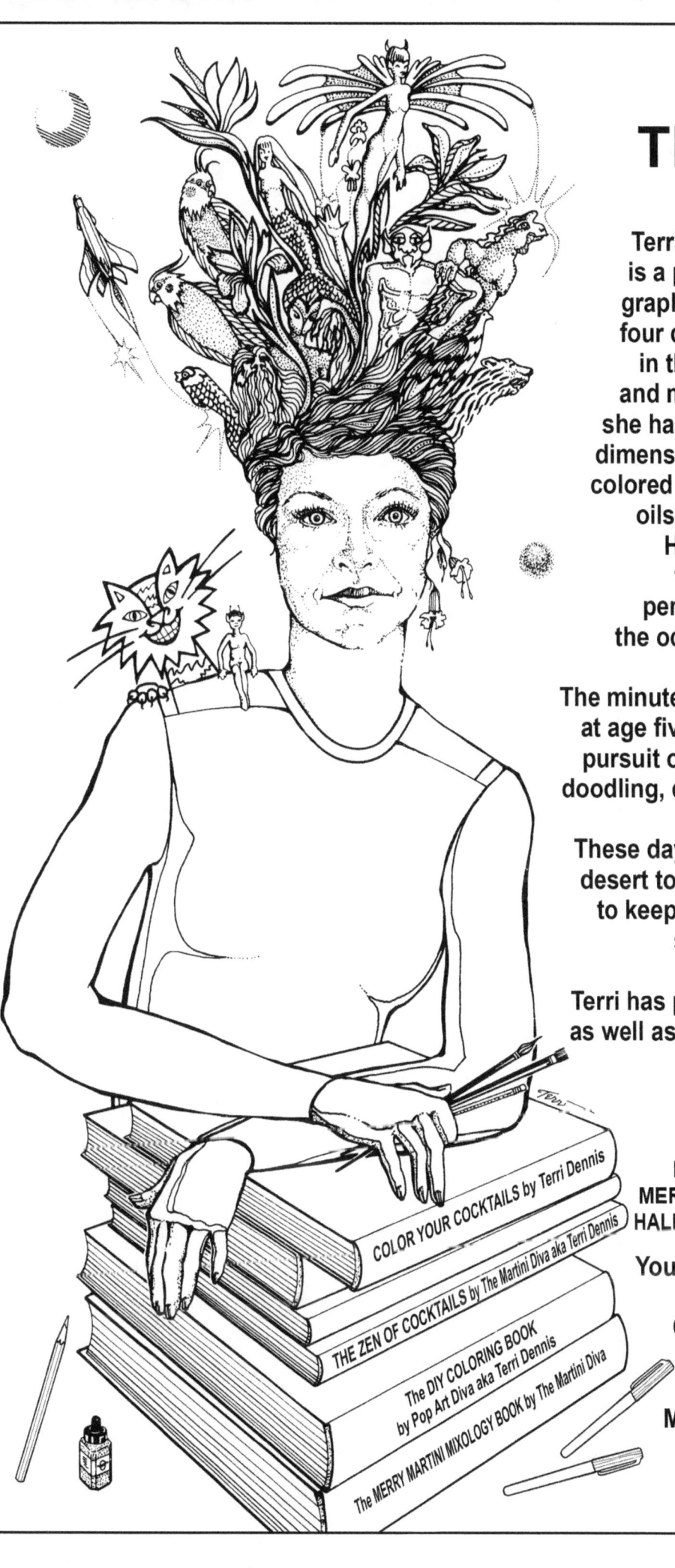

ABOUT
THE ARTIST

Terri Dennis, aka Pop Art Diva, is a professional illustrator and graphic artist/designer with over four decades of work experience in the publishing, advertising and marketing fields. In that time she has worked in every type of two dimensional media including pastels, colored pencils, markers, pen and ink, oils, acrylics and watercolors. Her favorite art mediums these days are colored pencils and watercolors with the occasional foray into acrylics.

The minute she was handed her first crayon at age five, Terri dedicated her life to the pursuit of creativity, color and the joy of doodling, drawing, illustration and painting.

These days she doodles and draws in the desert town of Tucson, Arizona and tries to keep her cat, Bailey, from eating or spilling stuff on her art.

Terri has published several cocktail books as well as other coloring books, including:

The DIY COLORING BOOK
The ZEN of COCKTAILS
COLOR YOUR COCKTAILS
MANDALAS & MOTIVATION
MERRY MARTIN MIXOLOGY BOOK
HALLOWEEN MARTINIS & MUNCHIES

You can find her other creative works at:
ColoringLifeHappy.Com
PopArtDiva.Com
ShopPopArtDiva.Com
MartiniDivaBoutique.Com
MartiniDiva.Com
TheMartiniDiva.Com

www.ingramcontent.com/pod-product-compliance
Lightning Source LLC
Chambersburg PA
CBHW080719190526
45169CB00006B/2441